Lost in the Rentharpian Hills

Carl Jacobi in 1936
"My car was new then, and I was new then."

Lost in the Rentharpian Hills
Spanning the Decades with Carl Jacobi

R. Dixon Smith

With Forewords by Robert Bloch and Joseph Payne Brennan

Bowling Green State University Popular Press
Bowling Green, Ohio 43403

Copyright © 1985 by Bowling Green State University Popular Press

Library of Congress Catalogue Card No.: 84-72634

ISBN: 0-87972-287-8 Clothbound
0-87972-288-6 Paperback

For John J. Koblas and Joseph A. West
Who pointed the way
And for Sally Mohr
A special lady who helped in special ways

For what shall it profit a man who liveth in a world of fantasy and a world of adventure but cannot tell one from another.

—Itsen Mie, *The Japanese Decalogue*

Contents

Acknowledgments

It is often said that writing a book is a solitary, lonely endeavor. If true, this book is an exception, for many friends—both mine and Carl Jacobi's—shared my enthusiasm and did much of my work for me. I wish to extend my grateful appreciation to the following individuals and institutions for their assistance and inspiration:

Arkham House Publishers, Inc. (Forrest D. Hartmann, Attorney and Roderic Meng, Operations); Steve Behrends; Fred Cook; J. Randolph Cox; Dr. Paul E. Cranefield; Gerry de la Ree; John R. Deveny; Estate of Robert E. Howard (Glenn Lord, **Agent**); Estate of Clark Ashton Smith (Richard E. Kuhn, Executor); Adam Granger; Rick Grimes; David D. Grothe; Kevin B. Hancer; Clark B. Hansen; S. Flensing Hlanith; Karin Hoyle; Allen J. Hubin; Scott Imes; Greg Ketter; E. P. Digges La Touche; Librairie des Champs-Elysees; Literary Manuscripts Collections of the Manuscripts Division of the University of Minnesota Libraries (Alan K. Lathrop, Curator); Walker Martin; Sherry Minnick; Richard H. Minter; James W. Morrison; Sam Moskowitz; Joseph Moudry, Jr.; Will Murray; *New Zealand Woman's Weekly* (Ann Haefeli, Secretary to Editor); Sandra Njoes; Peter Petzling; Robert M. Price; Leonard Robbins; Robert Sampson; San Francisco Academy of Comic Art (Bill Blackbeard, Director); Steve Sayles; Richard S. Smith; The State Historical Society of Wisconsin; Steven A. Stilwell; Tom and Kathy Stransky; James W. Thompson; Robert Weinberg; and Virgil Wilhite.

Thanks are due Harry H. Blade, Robert Bloch, Joseph Payne Brennan, Hugh B. Cave, Mary Elizabeth Counselman, Gordon R. Dickson, E. Hoffmann Price, Oliver Saari, Clifford D. Simak, and Donald Wandrei, for sharing recollections; Mary Elizabeth Counselman, John J. Koblas, and Joseph A. West, for the loan of letters from Carl Jacobi; Eric A. Carlson, for bibliographic and photographic assistance; Dennis K. Lien, for many hours of bibliographic research; R. Alain Everts, whose investment of time, care, substance, scholarship, and support was largely responsible for this book's having been written; Robert Bloch and Joseph Payne Brennan, for contributing forewords; R. Alain Everts, John J. Koblas, Dennis K. Lien, Sally Mohr, Philip J. Rahman, Thomas R.

Tietze, and Donald Wandrei, for reading the book in manuscript and making valuable suggestions; and my proofreader, Mary Ellen Gee, without whose editorial expertise many an inelegant phrase would have reached the printed page.

Finally, it is a special pleasure to acknowledge Carl Jacobi for many months of cooperation and assistance. His warmth, charm, humor, and generosity are quite genuine. He opened his files and offered me his mind, his recollections, his stubbornness, and—most important—his friendship. He too read the book in manuscript, made helpful suggestions, and proffered a precious commodity: encouragement.

R. Dixon Smith
St. Paul, Minnesota
October, 1984

Foreword by Robert Bloch

Now, regarding Carl—which I do, most highly. On the basis of just two face-to-face confrontations over a span of forty years, it would be presumptuous indeed for me to attempt any observations concerning his private *persona*, except to say that our meetings left me with very pleasant memories.

But my recollection of his work, read extensively and with great enjoyment over that same four-decade stretch of time, entitles me, I feel, to comment on Jacobi the writer; the *public persona*, as it were.

Or as it were not. Because, much to my sorrow, there has been all too little in the way of public activity on Carl's part; unlike the majority of his colleagues, he has never sought the limelight or courted favor with the media to obtain the degree of recognition he so deeply and definitely deserves. Of all *Weird Tales*' major contributors, he is probably the least known to a larger reading audience.

Thus it is with very special pleasure that I greet the publication of this biography and bibliography, in the hope that it will help to enhance acknowledgement and appreciation of a very special writer.

Foreword by Joseph Payne Brennan

I regret that I never had the pleasure of meeting Carl Jacobi in person. We have exchanged letters, however, and, through the medium of his carefully crafted stories, I look on Carl as an old and familiar friend.

For over a half century he has been publishing first-rate tales, some in the weird-horror tradition, some science fiction, and a fair number in other fields as well. All of Carl's stories are well written; the best are memorable. Stories like "Mive," "Revelations in Black" and "The Kite" come immediately to mind.

Carl's style is clear and sharp—never ornate or flamboyant. He is a dependable writer whose work wears well. His readers are loyal but they ought to be more widespread.

In my opinion he has not received the full plaudits he deserves. His books, *Revelations in Black, Portraits in Moonlight* and *Disclosures in Scarlet*, should be on the shelves of all dedicated writers and readers in the weird-supernatural genre.

The Golden Age of the Pulps, that legendary era of mass-produced thrills which flourished between the wars, began to thrive in the sensation-seeking Twenties. The public demanded hard-hitting escapist fare without frills, and colorful covers slugged it out at the newsstands in competition for the customer's small change. Descended from the earlier dime novels, such magazines as *Adventure, Argosy, Short Stories* and *The Blue Book Magazine* were among the biggest sellers. *Black Mask, Weird Tales, Railroad Stories, Cowboy Stories, Terror Tales, Top-Notch, Ghost Stories, Planet Stories, Thrilling Adventures, Dime Mystery Magazine, Oriental Stories, Amazing Stories* and a host of other titles were each devoted to a particular fiction field. Before its virtual extinction in the Fifties, the pulp industry was a $25,000,000 enterprise which spawned nearly 150 magazines per month, greedily devoured by 30,000,000 readers.

Carl Jacobi launched his writing career within such pages in 1928. The zest and vitality of his adventure yarns—"Smoke of the Snake," "Crocodile," "The Jade Scarlotti"—established him as one of America's most dependable fictioneers. His haunting tales of the supernatural and the macabre—"Moss Island," "Mive," "Revelations in Black," "Phantom Brass," "Carnaby's Fish," "The Corbie Door," "Portrait in Moonlight," "The La Prello Paper," "Matthew South and Company," "Witches in the Cornfield," "The Aquarium," "The Unpleasantness at Carver House," "The Singleton Barrier"—earned him a reputation as one of our leading writers of fantastic fiction.

How he came to be so regarded makes an interesting story in itself. This, then, is the Carl Jacobi story—his early interests and development, his successes and disappointments, and a career which spans more than five decades.

I

Not far from Lake Minnewashta in the Carver County outlands beyond Minneapolis, Minnesota, which would one day serve as the

3

setting for many of Carl Jacobi's most memorable macabre stories, Meta Todell Hoffman (1876-1965) and Minneapolis stock broker, bond salesman and investment counselor Richard Cleveland Jacobi (1872-1955) were wed on 30 October 1906. Both had moved to Minneapolis during childhood—she from Milwaukee and he from Cross Plains, Wisconsin.

Though he would not have admitted it, Richard Jacobi was a garrulous extrovert. One winter night, for instance, his sleep was interrupted well past midnight by the incessant howling of a neighborhood dog. Jacobi hurriedly threw on some clothes, waded through deep drifts of snow, clumped up to the neighbor's porch, and pounded on the door. "If you don't stop your dog from that infernal barking," he bellowed, "I'll shoot him myself!"[1] On another occasion, he gave a streetcar motorman a well-deserved tongue-lashing. Jacobi, who drove to work at the same time every day, became irritated by a motorman who seemed to take a fiendish delight in gunning the motor of his streetcar whenever the stop signs flashed "GO," thus forcing Jacobi to drop behind and lose his place in the flow of traffic. One morning, Jacobi rammed his vehicle into action, passed the streetcar, and screeched to a halt in the middle of the tracks. Slowly and calmly, he walked back to the motorman. "If you try that once more," he barked, "I'll report you to Thomas Lowry. Just remember that!"[2] Lowry, the millionaire owner of the city's streetcar system, was one of Jacobi's personal friends. The motorman never tried it again.

Richard and Meta's only child was born at their 3420 Stevens Avenue residence in Minneapolis on 10 July 1908. When Matie, as she preferred to be called, expressed the desire that her son be named Richard Carl, the boy's paternal grandfather, Carl August Jacobi (1846-1933), demanded that the child be named for him; at his insistence, the infant was christened Carl Richard Jacobi. He would become an introvert, inheriting his mother's retiring nature rather than the extroverted one of his father.

The family moved three times in the next six years, before buying their own home at 3717 4th Avenue South in 1914.[3] Carl Jacobi was to live in this house for the next fifty-seven years. Although his grandfather, who had emigrated from Treptow (a small town some eighty miles north of Berlin on the Tollense River), frequently quoted Goethe, Schiller and Lessing from memory in German in the Jacobi household, the youth was not raised bilingually; he did, however, read fantasy and juvenile adventure stories voraciously, including the Frank Merriwell books, the Tom

Richard Cleveland Jacobi

Meta Todell Hoffman

Swift series, the Boy Allies, the Submarine Boys, and, somewhat less appreciatively, the Rover Boys.

> I don't know when or where my first interest in weird and imaginative fiction began. I remember reading Jules Verne's *Twenty Thousand Leagues Under the Sea, The Mysterious Island, From the Earth to the Moon,* and *Hector Servadac (Off on a Comet).* And of course I read Poe and also *The Coming Race* by Edward Lord Bulwer-Lytton.[4]

His father, a great reader who had once served a hitch as a newspaper reporter on the *Minneapolis Times,* encouraged his son's aspirations as a writer. He and Carl frequently sat up at night, discussing various tales and plots the boy had been working on. The elder Jacobi soon bestowed upon his son the sobriquet which Carl later considered using as a professional pseudonym: Decatur De Koven.

> Father gave it to me half in jest, and I really don't know how he came upon that combination. I know, of course, that Reginald De Koven was the composer of one of Dad's favorite operettas, *Robin Hood.* And presumably Decatur came from Stephen B. Decatur, the American naval hero who fought the Barbary pirates in Tripoli. But why he should have put those two names together, unless it was for alliterative or euphonious reasons, I don't know.[5]

Throughout his early years, Jacobi never had to walk more than two blocks to school. His class was the last to graduate from the eighth grade at Bryant Grade School (later renamed Warrington and since razed), and the first to graduate from the ninth grade at Bryant Junior High, at a time when the concept of junior high schools was new to the Twin Cities. Here Carl began to sell handwritten "dime novels" for ten cents apiece to his classmates. Such was the inauspicious start of a literary career that has lasted nearly sixty years.

At Central High the following year, the school's literary magazine, *The Quest,* published his first complete tale, "The Runaway Box-Car" (December, 1924), about a freight car hurtling toward a collision with a passenger train; and successive issues featured "The Derelict" (May, 1925), which tells of an ancient caravel "driven by the winds of the seven seas for over three hundred years,"[6] in a style reminiscent of the sea stories of William Hope Hodgson and W. Clark Russell; "The Lost Tapestry"

Carl and his father
(6 April 1913)

Carl and his mother
(25 May 1913)

Carl and his grandfather,
Carl August Jacobi (1913)

Carl (17 May 1912)

"Carlie at the Wheel" (1915)

3717 4th Avenue South

(December, 1925), a macabre account of entombment in an ancient vault; "The War of the Sun Dials" (June, 1926), a fantasy yarn which explores the relativity of time; and a story for which its author is still justly proud: "Ultra" (December, 1926), a humorous sketch which pokes fun at the pretensions of modern art. It was during this period that Jacobi discovered the most prestigious of the fantasy pulp magazines, *Weird Tales*.

> I believe I was first introduced to *Weird Tales* by the issues which featured on their covers "The Stolen Body" by H.G. Wells, "Monsters of the Pit" by Paul S. Powers and "The Werewolf of Ponkert" by H. Warner Munn.[7]

II

After graduating from Central High in January, 1927, Jacobi enrolled at the University of Minnesota.

> I took German in my freshman year, and thought it would be a snap for me, as I often heard my father and grandfather speak German together. My grandfather nearly had a fit when I flunked the first semester flat. It was the only "F" I ever got in school. German is a difficult language to learn, much more so than Spanish, which I studied in high school.[8]

Carl once turned in, for a freshman composition assignment, the last story he had had published in *The Quest* while in high school; "Ultra" received an "A plus." In a subsequent quarter, one of his fellow students also turned in a previously written composition—not his own work, however, but a pulp story by Robert E. Howard. It too received a top grade. On the last day of the class, Jacobi approached the instructor. "I'd like you to know who I've been competing against," he announced. "A professional writer." "That often happens," was the professor's bemused reply.

During his college years, Carl night-clerked at a local hotel and worked on the editorial staff of *Ski-U-Mah*, the campus humor magazine.

> *Ski-U-Mah* was fashioned after the *Harvard Lampoon*. It had humorous sketches, jokes, cartoons, book reviews, theatrical and movie reviews, and interviews with people prominent on campus. One of the best issues we published while I was on the staff was a facsimile of *The New Yorker*. When I started on the magazine all I did was to contribute a few paragraph-long humorous stories. By the time I left (to take over

Carl's high-school graduation photo

Ray Bergin, Harry Blade, and Carl en route
to Canada (summer 1927)

a post on the *Minnesota Quarterly*), I had charge of the book reviews, theatrical reviews, and movie reviews, not all of which I wrote myself.[9]

Jacobi relates an amusing anecdote about film actor Victor Jory, who in 1928 was a matinee idol with the Bainbridge Players, a Minneapolis stock company which successfully staged such plays as *The Front Page, An American Tragedy, Rain, White Cargo, Dracula, The Green Hat* and Frederick Lonsdale's delightful comedy, *Aren't We All.*

I was very much stagestruck in those days. When Jory first opened in Minneapolis I was a student at the University, and having only morning classes at the time I used to sneak into the Shubert Theater and watch them rehearse. One time I was sitting in the back row of the empty theater and Jory saw me. He leaped over the footlights and ran up the aisle. "Was there something you wanted here?" he asked. I had to think fast so I replied, "I'm with the campus magazine *Ski-U-Mah*, and we'd like a picture of you for our coming issue." At the time this was pure fabrication, but Jory, sensing publicity, changed his attitude immediately. He took me up to the stage, introduced me to the rest of the cast, and even showed me the trap door in the stage floor (they were playing *Dracula* that week). Then he escorted me to a dressing room and after asking, "Are you decent?", introduced me to his leading lady, who at that time was a beautiful gal named Allys Dwyer. Days later I was walking down the street with a friend of mine, when he suddenly nudged me and said, "Do you know who that is ahead of us? That's the leading lady at the Shubert." When she came abreast of us she smiled and said, "How do you do, Mr. Jacobi?" You could have knocked my friend over with a feather.

Incidentally, when I had told Jory I was from the campus magazine and wanted a picture of him, it wasn't entirely a lie. He did give me a picture and it was used in a forthcoming issue. Later, of course, when Jory was here for his final season, I was a reporter on the *Minneapolis Star* and interviewed him.

About twenty years after this, Jory's daughter was in Minneapolis, and through the column of *Tribune* writer George Grim appealed to any readers to send her programs of plays in which her father had appeared. Seems he had neglected to save them and she wanted to give him "one or two" as a birthday present. I not only had a few; I had all of them and she wrote a very appreciative letter when I sent them to her.[10]

In the summer of 1927, Carl and high-school chums Harry Blade and Ray Bergin set out for Canada on a one-week camping trip. Heading north one night toward International Falls,

Minnesota, they found themselves caught in a driving rainstorm without headlights after a fuse blew and they discovered they had no spares. Undaunted, Jacobi devised an amusing solution. While Bergin drove, Carl hung out the window, pointing his flashlight at the road. In that fashion, they managed to make their way to Canada without further mishap, and pitched their tent at Pither's Point near Rainy Lake outside Fort Frances, Ontario. A few days later, the tent developed a leak during another downpour, and the boys prepared for the worst. Then they remembered the flapjacks they had thrown away earlier that day. Retrieving them, they quickly patched the hole in the tent—a somewhat unsightly, but satisfactory, solution. They spent the rest of the week fishing, discussing Lindbergh's recent solo flight across the Atlantic, and meeting girls. One who caught Carl's fancy was a winsome lass from Eveleth, Minnesota, whom he later squired to a play at the Shubert Theater.

Jacobi is fond of recalling an embarrassing incident which occurred when he attended a Shubert Production of Ben Hecht's and Charles MacArthur's *The Front Page*. Finding it necessary to leave the theater before the play's finale, Carl was making a discreet exit when suddenly, half-way up the aisle, he heard his name bellowed from the stage. A startled Jacobi froze in his tracks. It was a full minute before it dawned on him that "Jacobi" was a character in the play.

Carl was working for *Ski-U-Mah* during his sophomore year when he received a telephone call from his mother, informing him that his detective story "Rumbling Cannon" (featuring the elusive burglar Stephen Benedict) had been accepted by *Secret Service Stories*, a pulp which specialized in tales of international intrigue. He had asked her to open all his mail from publishers. "When I got this news, I was no good at any of my classes for the rest of the day," Jacobi recalls. "I walked on air."[11] Oddly enough, he never received a cent for the first story he sold; *Secret Service Stories* folded soon after its September, 1928, issue, containing "Rumbling Cannon," hit the newstands.

Shortly thereafter, the faculty advisor of Central High's *The Quest* called to ask for a post-graduate contribution. Carl furnished "Moss Island" (May, 1930), a claustrophobic chiller about an irruption of mutant moss growth, which was later republished in the Winter, 1932, issue of *Amazing Stories Quarterly*; in 1947 it resurfaced in Jacobi's first hardbound collection for Arkham House, *Revelations in Black*. Similarly, one of Jacobi's best early efforts,

"Mive," an effective tale of enormous, carnivorous butterflies discovered in a murky, primeval bog, was originally written for the University's literary magazine, *Minnesota Quarterly*. When Duluth's Margaret Culkin Banning, one of Minnesota's most prominent authors, selected it as the best creative-writing achievement in a University-sponsored short-story contest, Jacobi was quickly offered, and as quickly accepted, an editorial position on the *Minnesota Quarterly* staff. After its publication there (Fall, 1928), "Mive" appeared in the January, 1932, issue of *Weird Tales*; it too was later reprinted in Jacobi's premiere collection for Arkham House in 1947. The *Minnesota Quarterly* also ran three of his detective yarns: "The Borgian Chandelier" (Fall, 1929) and "Enter Stephen Benedict" (Winter, 1930), two more accounts of the elusive gentleman thief, and "The Masked Orange" (Spring, 1930), in which Benedict is mentioned.

That Jacobi had skillfully captured the pervading ambience of gloom prevalent in the work of Edgar Allan Poe in the dusky, melancholic opening passages of "Mive" ("The day was certainly anything but ideal; a raw wind whipping in from the south, and a leaden sky typical of early September lent anything but an inviting aspect to those rolling Rentharpian hills.")[12] was not overlooked by H. P. Lovecraft (1890-1937), America's most celebrated fantasist since Poe and Ambrose Bierce. In December, 1931, Lovecraft wrote to fellow pulp writer August W. Derleth (1909-1971) of Sauk City, Wisconsin, and remarked, "It has the pervasive, insidious atmosphere so discouragingly lacking in almost all cheap weird fiction."[13] Two months later, Jacobi received an encouraging letter from Lovecraft (dated 27 February 1932), congratulating him on the appearance of "Mive" in *Weird Tales*:

> ... "Mive" pleased me immensely, & I told Wright that I was glad to see at least one story whose weirdness of incident was made convincing by adequate emotional preparation & suitably developed atmosphere. Most of the stuff in the cheap weird magazines is utterly & irredeemably flat because of the lack of any substance to lend a semblance of actuality to the extravagant & over-crowded incidents. I also read "The Coach on the Ring," & wish the editor had had the discernment to let the original title stand. Many things in this tale captivated me exceedingly, though as you realize it was a little nearer the popular magazine formula than "Mive." I hope to see the other items of yours which you mention—& congratulate you sincerely on your success in making varied placements. Your versatility is decidedly greater than my own for I can never hit

Carl (about 1930)

Carl (late 1930s)

the popular formula well enough to land anywhere but in *Weird Tales*....

Derleth spoke very highly of your work & future promise, & admiringly heralded "Mive" long before it appeared .... Possibly you also know my brilliant young friend Donald Wandrei, of your own Twin Cities.[14]

Indeed he did. One of Jacobi's closest friends during his undergraduate years was fellow student and fantasy writer Donald A. Wandrei (1908-   ) of St. Paul, a friend of Lovecraft's since 1926 and a frequent contributor of stories and poems to the *Minnesota Quarterly*. Long after the October, 1927, appearance of his most famous story, "The Red Brain" (submitted as "In the Twilight of Time"), in *Weird Tales*, Wandrei was instrumental in founding Arkham House with August Derleth in 1939. The Sauk City, Wisconsin, publishing concern has specialized in hardbound editions of the works of Lovecraft, Clark Ashton Smith, Robert E. Howard, William Hope Hodgson and other macabre writers.

Jacobi had wanted to meet Derleth for some time, and told Wandrei in December, 1930, that he had become addicted to the Wisconsin writer's Solar Pons adventures, those popular Sherlock Holmes pastiches which had been running in *The Dragnet*. "I know the chap who wrote them," Wandrei said. "His name is Derleth and he'll be in Minneapolis in a few weeks. Would you care to meet him?"[15] When Jacobi eagerly assented, Wandrei arranged the festivities, which took place over dinner at the Rainbow Cafe in Minneapolis. The three writers spent the night discussing imaginative fiction over coffee, talking especially of Lovecraft and the recently published *Weird Tales* novelette, "The Horror from the Hills," penned by fellow fantasist Frank Belknap Long (1901-   ). Jacobi recalls the meeting:

My first impression of Derleth was that of size. He was a big man and seemed to radiate physical strength as well as mental. Many writers are on the delicate side or at least are introverts, and it seemed strange to come upon a man in his profession who looked as though he would be more comfortable doing things with his hands.[16]

This encounter paved the way for an exchange of letters which would last almost forty years. Their correspondence began a year later, when Derleth sent Jacobi a message full of praise for "Mive," which had just appeared in *Weird Tales*. In his letter, Derleth noted:

You certainly hit upon a plot every *Weird Tales* reader and writer is glad to welcome—something out of the ordinary. I had a letter from Clark Ashton Smith only this morning in which he comments on the January issue, saying that " 'Mive,' for sheer unusualness, certainly stands out," etc.[17]

III

Carl Jacobi finished his studies at the University of Minnesota, where he had majored in English Literature and Composition and minored in Journalism, in December, 1930. Although he was still living at home, and would continue to live there for the next four decades, he supported himself for a while by taking a turn at newspaper reporting on the *Minneapolis Star*, where he also reviewed plays and worked as a rewrite man.

On one assignment when I was still very green in the journalism field, I interviewed a dentist doing graduate work at the University who had recently come from Australia. During the course of the interview he mentioned the Dingo dog, and declared he had proof that this animal many times kills its prey with sharp, needle-like wounds at the base of the throat. Now the play *Dracula* was playing at a local stock company in Minneapolis, and the city editor, without compunction, changed my story to read that Bram Stoker, the author of *Dracula*, had got his basic idea for the book from the predatory activities of the Dingo. It had absolutely no basis in fact, of course, and it infuriated me, though the *Star* in those days never used a by-line and I thus couldn't be held responsible for such blatant lies.[18]

With college behind him, Jacobi settled down to writing in earnest. He quickly sold "The Coach on the Ring" to *Ghost Stories*, which published it as "The Haunted Ring" (December, 1931-January, 1932). This Jacobi classic, an eerie East Prussian tale about a spectral coach and its hooded coachman, was originally scheduled to run under the pseudonym of James K. Vermont, but at the last minute Carl changed his mind and dashed off a letter to *Ghost Stories*, asking them to substitute his own by-line.

Jacobi recalls the circumstances which led, in the early summer of 1930, to the composition of one of his most celebrated stories:

... I was driving down the Rockford road west of Minneapolis; it was a beautiful moonlit night and the countryside was bright as day. Suddenly I came upon a farm which riveted my attention. Three life-sized statues stood at attention by the roadside. In the farmyard was what appeared to be an old stone fountain with images carved on its sides. And on either side of the farmhouse door like silent sentries stood two more life-sized statues. Extending to the west end of the property for apparently no reason at all was a brick wall, the top of which was ornamented with more carvings. In the moonlight the scene made a profound impression on me, and I gave no thought to the fact that the farm in all probability had been taken over by someone whose former occupation had been a stonecutter. I only know that the scene served as the germ for what was to be perhaps my most successful fantasy story, "Revelations in Black."[19]

In 1931, after it had initially been rejected by *Strange Tales* and *Ghost Stories*, Jacobi sent the manuscript to Farnsworth Wright (1888-1940), editor of *Weird Tales*.

I never met Farnsworth Wright personally. One of the marked things about his letters is that they never bore a written signature. He suffered from Parkinson's disease and writing was difficult for him.

Wright was an astute editor, but he had several stock phrases he used to reject a manuscript. One of these was, "I find the enclosed story very unconvincing." When I first sent him "Revelations in Black" he rejected it. Months later he wrote me a letter asking, "Do you still have that story about the strange garden with the twenty-six blue jays? That story haunts me and if you still have it I should like to see it again."[20]

Jacobi resubmitted the story, and was back in the pages of *Weird Tales* in April, 1933. "Revelations in Black"—carefully crafted, imaginatively handled, written with economy, subtlety and restraint—remains one of the most memorable tales of vampirism ever published; in addition to providing the title for his first Arkham House collection in 1947, it has often been reprinted in both hardbound and paperback anthologies, and has appeared in numerous foreign translations, including French and Swedish.

IV

Jacobi soon realized that he preferred freelancing to the regular hours of a steady job, and left the *Star*. He rented an uptown office on the corner of Lake Street and Lyndale Avenue, placed his typewriter and a ream of paper on the desk, rolled up his sleeves and became a full-fledged fictioneer. When one considers that pulp yarns were "churned out by writers needing a quick sale, marketed by companies seeking a quick profit, and bought by readers demanding a quick escape,"[21] it should hardly be surprising that writing for the pulps was a precarious existence at best. These were the days when pulp authors "had to make a typewriter smoke in order to keep eating,"[22] for rates were low; generally ranging from ½¢ to 1½¢ per word, penny-a-word rates were fairly standard, payable either upon acceptance or upon publication (post-publication payments frequently characterized none-too-solvent operations, but established leaders employed the practice as well). As a result, those who earned their livelihood in the pulp industry were forced to sell new copy as fast as they could grind it out in order to survive. Considering the breathless pace with which most pulp writers dashed off their products, it is astonishing that anything of lasting quality was created. Several writers, however, including Dashiell Hammett, Raymond Chandler, H. P. Lovecraft, Clark Ashton Smith, Robert E. Howard, William Hope Hodgson, Frank Belknap Long, Donald Wandrei, Hugh B. Cave, E. Hoffmann Price, August Derleth, Mary Elizabeth Counselman, Henry S. Whitehead, H. Russell Wakefield, David H. Keller, Robert Bloch, Joseph Payne Brennan, Ray Bradbury, and Carl Jacobi did some of their best work for the pulps; their tales are reprinted because they still hold up well.

Jacobi quickly established himself as a struggling word merchant in the manuscript mill, and managed to earn a modest living during the Depression. To be successful, a pulp writer had to sell to as many markets as possible. Jacobi maintained versatility and did not confine himself to the fantasy field. His stock list of available manuscripts included adventure stories, historical romances, mysteries, detective thrillers, and an occasional railroad yarn or western, and they were published by the dozens; but his efforts in the genre of fantasy—weird, macabre, supernatural and science fiction—held more promise of literary durability. As he habitually started stories the minute a mood or idea struck him, only to discover later that the denouement entirely escaped him, Jacobi quickly tossed them aside, and to this day he retains a large collection of unfinished manuscripts.

Jacobi's work appeared six times within the pages of *Weird Tales* during the next five years. A snowbound corpse refuses to accept its mortality in "The Last Drive" (June, 1933); rapiers glisten in the slanting sunlight of a twentieth-century museum as Louis XIII's guardsmen live again in "A Pair of Swords" (August, 1933); an accursed North Borneo walking stick, "The Cane" (April, 1934), forces its owner to commit murder; through hypnotism and telepathy, "The Satanic Piano" (May, 1934) transposes musical inspiration into its own malignant compositions;[23] there's something on the other side of that wall, in the Royalton Manor marsh, that's struggling to get out, in a frightful tale of harpies entitled "The Face in the Wind" (April, 1936);[24] and in "The Devil Deals" (April, 1938), a professional cardsharp encounters a deadly deck of cards fashioned by a fourteenth-century Spanish sorcerer.

Leo Margulies, editor-in-chief of the Thrilling Publication chain, bought eight of Jacobi's weird-menace yarns for *Thrilling Mystery* during this period. A greed-crazed maniac thirsts for human sacrifice in the horror-shrouded novelette "Death Rides the Plateau" (May, 1936); a grim harbinger of death soars over the East Borneo jungle near Samarinda in "Satan's Kite" (June, 1937); a decapitated warrior god stalks a South Seas freighter with his "Head in His Hands" (November, 1937); embalmed corpses litter Jacobi's ghastliest concoction as "The Bells Toll Blood" (January, 1938); in another novelette, an ancient curse concerning sinister corbies hovers over the "House of the Ravens" (September, 1938); a beauty salon provides an unlikely setting for hair-raising schemes in "Murder for Medusa" (January, 1939); "Death's Outpost" (May, 1939) tells of the *Sangumenke*, a secret society among New Guinea natives; and the novelette "Flight of the Flame Fiend" (July, 1939) proffers a stone idol with terrifyingly destructive fingers of fire.

Thrilling Wonder Stories, also edited by Leo Margulies, ran three of Jacobi's science-fiction tales. "The World in a Box" (February, 1937), written in 1928, about the time he produced "Mive," is one of Jacobi's earliest and most undistinguished stories, and has a reporter reduced in size and propelled into a miniature, prehistoric world; in "Cosmic Teletype" (October, 1938), a Minnesotan with a silver plate in his brain receives extraterrestrial messages from an expeditionary force bent on conquering Earth; and in "The War of the Weeds" (February, 1939), inhabitants of a dying planet attempt to destroy Earth's population by infesting Carver County, Minnesota, with an undulating plant growth which causes insanity. In *Strange Stories*, a Lisbon optician's telescope affords glimpses into a foggy world of ruined edifices in "Sagasta's Last" (August, 1939), a *Weird Tales* reject whose title was suggested by August Derleth; while a crudely fashioned wooden carving resembling a rat begins to kill and mutilate in "Spawn of Blackness" (October, 1939).

Other tales published during this period were "The Tomb from Beyond" (*Wonder Stories*, November, 1933), a favorite of H. P.

Lovecraft's, concerning the shipment of a strange, ornamented casket from the mysterious sunken city of Dras; "Satan's Roadhouse" (*Terror Tales*, October, 1934), a diverting weird-menace novelette festooned with hanging corpses and a twenty-foot python; "The Man from Makassar" (*Marvel Tales*, Summer, 1935), a fan magazine contribution (also turned down by *Weird Tales*) about a dead man's vengeance on the Java Sea; and "Wings for a Monster" (*The Phantom Detective*, October, 1937), a semi-weird detective yarn featuring, of all things, a flying ape. *Wild West Stories and Complete Novel Magazine* ran Jacobi's only published western, "The Bantam Ben Hur" (March, 1934), a delightfully humorous little gem in which every western town sponsors a rodeo, but only one a chariot race. He had to rewrite the ending three times before *Railroad Stories* published "Phantom Brass" (August, 1934), an impressively haunting tale of the supernatural reminiscent of Sir Arthur Conan Doyle. Another railroad yarn, "Train Kidnap," appeared in the December 21, 1935, issue of the *Toronto Star Weekly*. Jacobi made his first sale to the slicks when *Maclean's Magazine* in Toronto published "Loaded Coupling" (February 1, 1936), a third railroad story; it was followed by "Ticket to Nowhere" (*Airlanes*, May, 1936), a short-short about a salesman whose dream of traveling in Europe comes true. Slick-paper magazines, such as *The Saturday Evening Post, Ladies' Home Journal, Woman's Home Companion, Collier's, Redbook* and *Cosmopolitan*, were more prestigious publications than the pulps, and paid correspondingly higher rates—often as much as 7¢ a word.

Jacobi continued to pound out new material for a variety of markets, confident that he'd land an average of one acceptance for every three manuscripts on first submission (or, when some of the work was haphazard, one out of four). Undaunted by the stories that bounced, he quickly devised a clever means of circumventing such rejections. When Farnsworth Wright sent him a letter of nonacceptance, with instructions to rewrite most of the tale, Jacobi frequently held it untouched for several weeks or months, and then returned it with a cover letter stating that all the requested changes had been made. Wright nearly always accepted the story on its second submission; Jacobi claims that this system worked well with many editors.

Among the writers who continued to provide him with sources of inspiration were Edgar Allan Poe, H. P. Lovecraft (whose "The Rats in the Walls" is a favorite of Jacobi's), Arthur Machen, M. R. James, Algernon Blackwood, J. Sheridan Le Fanu, August Derleth and Hugh B. Cave; Rafael Sabatini, the Italian-born British author of swashbuckling historical romances which thrilled millions of readers (Jacobi's favorites are *Scaramouche* and *Captain Blood*); and Alexandre Dumas, Rudyard Kipling, Sir Arthur Conan Doyle, Maurice Leblanc, W. Somerset Maugham and Daphne du Maurier.

Jacobi recalls nearly four decades of correspondence with August Derleth:

> Every three weeks or month I received a letter from him, and the correspondence was to become a part of my life.
>
> One of the strange things about the Derleth letters was their promptness. No matter how busy he was nor how long I waited before replying, I could always be sure that he would answer without fail in three days, the time it took for a letter to reach me. We rarely discussed anything but "shop talk," the literary markets, writing projects which he had on hand. He never discussed personal matters, or at least rarely, and it was a long time before I knew he had a sister.
>
> In later years, much of this correspondence had to do with sales of my stories, reprint rights and translations of stories of mine for which he had acted as agent.[25]
>
> I owe a great deal to him. He criticized and edited my early weird tales, he kept me posted on the literary trends and markets, he consoled me during periods of "no acceptance," and he published my first book.[26]

In August, 1930, Jacobi struck up a friendship with Hugh B. Cave (1910-   ) of Pawtucket, Rhode Island, the British-born writer whose contributions to *Weird Tales* included "The Crawling Curse," "The Watcher in the Green Room," "The Brotherhood of Blood" and "The Ghoul Gallery." Their exchange of letters continues after more than fifty years. Relates Cave:

> I can't recall when Carl Jacobi and I began corresponding. Either I wrote to him about one of his stories that impressed me, or he wrote to say he liked one of mine. No matter. It was the start of a friendship that has grown through the years and continues today, even though we have never come face to face.
>
> I kept all his letters, but the early ones were lost in a fire some years ago, along with copies of all my early stories.
>
> This I know: we used to read each other's published tales with even more care than the editors must have read them, and the comments and criticisms we sent each other unquestionably influenced our future work. "This isn't one of your best," Carl would say, gently pointing out why. When he liked something, he would be just as specific. It helped. It still does, for we still do it.[27]

Jacobi's long list of correspondents included such enthusiastic supporters as H. P. Lovecraft of Providence, Rhode Island, with whom he exchanged letters until Lovecraft's death in 1937; Robert E. Howard (1906-1936) of Cross Plains, Texas, with whom he corresponded until Howard took his own life; and Clark Ashton Smith (1893-1961), the renowned fantasist from Auburn, California. But the letters he treasures most came in the Forties from Rafael Sabatini (1875-1950), who lived at Clifford, Herefordshire, England, whenever he wasn't skiing in Switzerland. Sabatini's penmanship "was so minute it looked as if it had been done with an electric stylus,"[28] and Jacobi needed a magnifying glass to decipher his handwriting.

Concerning another literary influence, Jacobi recalls:

> I became interested in Maurice Leblanc when I read the first of his Arsene Lupin books. When I tried to get more of the adventures of this gentleman burglar I found it almost impossible. Even then many of these books were either out of print or simply not sold in this country. But they fascinated me, probably because he was a worthy opponent of Doyle's Sherlock Holmes. The publishers couldn't use the name Sherlock Holmes so they changed it, sometimes to Holmlock Shears and sometimes to Herlock Sholmes. I wasn't alone in this fascination. In his autobiography Conan Doyle relates how he once went to his club in London for a game of billiards. He had been playing for an hour or so when the piece of chalk he used to chalk his cue suddenly broke open. In it was a minute piece of paper bearing the words, "Arsene Lupin's compliments to Sherlock Holmes."
> Arsene Lupin was a gentleman thief, much more believable than E. W. Hornung's Raffles, who makes sport of Sherlock Holmes whenever the English detective and he are pitted against each other. For his creation, Maurice Leblanc was made a Chevalier of the Legion of Honor.[29]

V

One of Jacobi's specialties throughout the years has been meticulously researched adventure yarns with exotic locales.[30]

> About this time I became interested in the Dutch portion of the island of Borneo. Hugh Cave had been writing stories of the British side of the island and had created the memorable outpost Tsiang House and the fictitious river, the Molo. But the Dutch side of the island had received little attention. I managed to obtain the vague location of a Dutch military garrison where

forty men were stationed. It was in the heart of the head-hunting country, in a district then marked on all maps as "unexplored," and very little was known about it.

Mail was not what it is today. My letter to the commanding officer requesting background information went by train to San Francisco, across the Pacific to Singapore where it was transferred to a coastal freighter, and then around to the east coast of Borneo to a port called Tandjong-Selor. From there it went up the Kayan River. I had routed the letter to Samarinda and up the Mahakam River, but the Mahakam was no longer navigable. Anyway, the letter went upriver by military transport in soldered tins so the dampness would not get it. When it reached the *onderafdeeling* (district) of Apo Kayan, the commanding officer was most obliging.[31]

He promptly forwarded geographic information, ethnic lore and a wealth of detail, which Jacobi used to good effect when he wrote "Sumpitan," "Quarry," "Spider Wires," "Dead Man's River," "East of Samarinda," "Trial by Jungle," "Hamadryad Chair" and "The Jade Scarlotti."

Another exotic setting was Ambunti, a lonely police outpost 230 miles up the Sepik River in northeast New Guinea. Jacobi spotted it on a map, took a chance with the address, and posted a letter to the officer in charge.

Two white men and fifteen native troopers are stationed there in what seems to be the world's jumping-off spot. It's wild country, right in the heart of head-hunting region, surrounded by low swampy jungle, uncivilized natives, millions of malarial mosquitos and crocodiles. The chap who answered my letter was the assistant district officer, an Australian, I presume, and—so he claimed—a former journalist. Anyway he outdid himself in furnishing background information, local color, tribal names, etc. Promised to furnish more detail upon request and asked that I pass on to him a few copies of *Esquire*. The letter traveled to the coast, to a port called Madang, by a Chinese pinnace.[32]

"Death's Outpost" was inspired by this letter.

"Tiger Island," "Death On Tin Can," "Holt Sails the 'San Hing' " and "Captain Jinx" were set in Sumatra, the Unfederated Malay States, and the Java, Arafura and Sulu Seas. Jacobi always supplemented his research with requests for information from American vice-consuls, conservators of forests, harbor masters, customs officials and ship captains. "Twenty-two below here yesterday," he wrote Derleth one winter evening, "and me writing about the South China Sea."[33]

His tales of the Caribbean buccaneers—"Black Lace" and "The Commission of Captain Lace"—required even more rigorous accuracy:

> ...the history of England and Spain, the latitude and longitude of the smaller islands, the island ports, British Port Royal, French Tortuga, Spanish Porto Bello, the types of ships and the guns they carried and a thousand incidentals, costumes in the various walks of life, side arms, rapiers, the whole art of fencing. And of course the biographies of the pirates, Morgan, Edward Teach, called Blackbeard, and the cruelest and most bloodthirsty of them all, a gentleman called L'Ollinais. Here my correspondent was Rafael Sabatini, who, because of his Captain Blood stories, was well acquainted with the area.[34]

Such exactitude demanded time; most pulp writers seldom bothered, and it showed. As Jacobi wrote to Derleth:

> I was browsing through a Sabatini romance the other day. The setting of the story was listed as the Albuquerque Keys, northwest of Porto Bello in latitude twelve degrees north, eighty-five degrees west longitude. Somebody pulled a boner, for that location is in the middle of Nicaragua, dry land. Who said I didn't know my West Indies![35]

Thrilling Adventures, edited by Leo Margulies, soon became one of Jacobi's most lucrative markets for adventure stories, running seven of them during the next several years. The novelette "Black Passage" (May, 1936) tells of a gun-running operation off the New Guinea coast aboard a plague ship that has broken quarantine; in "Spider Wires" (January, 1937), which appeared under the nom de plume of Jackson Cole, a murderer fleeing from justice in the Dutch East Borneo jungle attempts to steal five sacred emeralds from a native totem; in the same issue, a man falsely accused of murder pursues the real killer through the Borneo jungle and up "Dead Man's River"; South Pacific poachers locate a virgin bed of pearl oysters in Dutch waters off "Tiger Island" (May, 1937);[36] in "Balu Guns" (September, 1937), a British Secret Service operative tracks down smuggled rifles in Baluchistan (then the northwest frontier of India, and today a Pakistani province); a young ethnologist travels up the Mahakam River into the Borneo interior to find a lost gold deposit, and is pursued by two white renegades out to steal the lode, in "Trial by Jungle" (September, 1939); and "The Twenty-One Crescents" (November, 1939) is a novelette of espionage and intrigue in Baluchistan.

Complete Stories took "Crocodile" (April 30, 1934), a Borneo tale of murder and retribution; "Jungle Wires" (September 24, 1934), about a gun-running operation at a Dutch East Borneo telegraph relay outpost stationed far up the Mahakam River;[37] "Three Brass Cubes" (January 28, 1935), which has a photographer beset by killers and fierce Marri warriors in Baluchistan;[38] and "Deceit Post" (February 18, 1935), in which Borneo trader Joe Klay outsmarts a murderer who tries to steal rare motion-picture footage of a lost Taoist tribe. *Top-Notch* published "Smoke of the Snake" (January, 1934), a Borneo "weird" set in a Samarinda opium den, wherein an elderly Oriental avenges his daughter's death; "Letter of Dismissal" (October, 1934), in which a young officer in the Dutch Borneo colonial service, facing dishonorable discharge for insubordination, prevents a native uprising and the looting of a diamond mine; and "Sumpitan" (October, 1935), which showcases a battle to the death between a Royal Netherlands Indies officer and a native chieftain with Sumpitan blowguns. *The Skipper* offered "East of Samarinda" (July, 1937), a novelette about a spy organization near the headwaters of the Mahakam River in Borneo's head-hunting country; and "Death On Tin Can" (December, 1937), a South Pacific tale of rivalry among pearl thieves. *Short Stories*, edited by Dorothy McIlwraith, served up "Holt Sails the 'San Hing' " (January 25, 1938), which tells of a rajah's smuggled riches and mutiny off the coast of the Unfederated Malay States; and "Leopard Tracks" (July 10, 1938), a novelette about diamond smuggling in the rubber-rich Sepitang jungle of British North Borneo. Other action yarns were "Quarry" (*Dime Adventure Magazine,* December, 1935), concerning the relentless pursuit of a murderer up the Mahakam River and through the Borneo jungle; "A Film in the Bush" (*Doc Savage,* September, 1937), in which a motion picture provides the key to the location of a platinum deposit in the Apo Kayan district of Dutch East Borneo; and "Drowned Destiny" (*12 Adventure Stories,* March, 1939), a terror tale about deep sea divers in the South Pacific.

VI

In the mid-Thirties, Jacobi built a summer cabin on Lake Minnewashta, some twenty-five miles west of Minneapolis in rural Carver County. He and Harry Blade bought two lots and had identical cabins built by a contractor according to their specifications.

Later we purchased eight additional and adjoining lots. At that

Carl's and Harry Blade's cabins under construction (mid-1930s)

Carl and Alma Eide, whom he dated
frequently in the 1930s

Best Man at Harry and Lois Blade's wedding
(20 August 1938)

> time the area of Red Cedar Point on Lake Minnewashta wasn't
> built up as it is today. Although electricity was available, Harry
> and I had kerosene lamps and more or less gloried in the rustic
> back-to-nature location. The cabins originally had only one
> room each, but we later added porches, etc. I did a lot of the
> construction work myself, though I'm anything but handy with
> tools.[39]
> I built the place as a studio where I could write in the quiet I
> thought was conducive to creative work. I should have known
> better. As a former newspaper reporter on a metropolitan daily, I
> was accustomed to the noise, bustle and confusion of the "city
> room." The cabin was too quiet.[40]

He wrote but one story there, during a blizzard which blocked all
roads to Minneapolis. Finding himself short of firewood, he
pounded the typewriter to keep warm, and produced "Prisoners of
Vibration." It didn't sell.

When his interest in foreign locales began to flag, Jacobi turned
to his own back yard for fresh inspiration. Using the Carver County
settings of Chaska, Chanhassen and Victoria, he fashioned "The
War of the Weeds" and, many years later, nearly a dozen additional
fantasy tales.

> ... I wrote "The Unpleasantness at Carver House," which
> concerned an after-death situation in a strange old mansion;
> "The Cocomacaque," which had to do with a bank robbery in the
> village of Victoria, three miles from my cabin; "The Singleton
> Barrier," which told of an odd brick wall at neighboring Lake
> Bavaria; "Test Case," which had to do with an alien invasion in
> the town of Waconia, twenty-five miles west; "The Pit," which
> concerned an old Indian burial mound near Chaska, the Carver
> County seat; "McIver's Fancy," which told of a series of murders
> and a sleepwalker in the same vicinity; and "The Black
> Garden," about a strange woman out of the past who got off the
> bus at Cologne, another small village in the area.[41]

The fashionably attired, pipe-smoking Jacobi became one of the
earliest members and staunchest supporters of the Minneapolis
Fantasy Society, which was formed when science-fiction writer
Clifford D. Simak (1904-) quit his position as managing editor of a
newspaper in Brainerd, Minnesota, and moved to the Twin Cities in
1939 to take a job as copyreader on the *Minneapolis Star*. After
meeting Jacobi and other local authors, Simak suggested that they
form a fraternal organization of fantasy fans. This they did, and
through Simak's guidance, the group began to publish a regular
journal, *The Fantasite*. The first meeting of the MFS was held at

Clifford D. Simak, Donald Wandrei,
and Carl (23 January 1942)

Seated, left to right: Arden Benson
(with mascot Squanchfoot), Charles
Albertson, Oliver Saari, Ken Peterson,
and Sam Russell; standing, left to right;
John Chapman, Clifford D. Simak,
Carl, Cyril Eggum, Douglas Blakely,
and Phil Bronson (10 January 1941)

Donald Wandrei and Carl (21 September 1941)

Clifford Simak's home on 28 November 1940. Besides Simak and Jacobi, members included Donald Wandrei (whose "Colossus" remains one of Jacobi's favorite science-fiction stories), Finnish-born Oliver Saari (who wrote science fiction for *Astounding Stories*), Gordon R. Dickson (whom Saari had met at the University of Minnesota), Poul Anderson, Morris Scott Dollens, John Chapman, Sam Russell, Phil Bronson, Bob Wansbrough, John Gergen, Dale Rostomily, Manson Brackney, Arthur Osterlund, Charles Albertson, Frances Blomstrand, Paul Koppes, Rodman Allen, Ken Peterson, Doug Blakely and Arden Benson. Although they were all addicted to classical music and enjoyed listening to the newest recordings at their frequent gatherings, they also discussed old times (chiefly Jacobi and Wandrei), reviewed the latest pulps, hashed over new story ideas and made recordings of some of their proceedings for posterity: one of these was Donald Wandrei's talk on Farnsworth Wright and *Weird Tales*, which was waxed at the YMCA on 21 September 1941.

As a result of their association in the Minneapolis Fantasy Society, Jacobi and Simak collaborated on two science-fantasy stories, "The Street That Wasn't There" and "The Cat That Had Nine Lives." Jacobi told Derleth how they wrote the former:

> I had the idea. We discussed it. He wrote the first draft, but the ending turned out badly. I did it over, added what I thought was necessary and cut a good deal.[42]

But although both tales were accepted by *Comet*, only one was published, for the magazine folded shortly after the appearance of "The Street That Wasn't There" in July, 1941. Fearful that he and Simak wouldn't be paid, Jacobi contacted the Authors' Guild. As he was an active member of this national organization, the Guild intervened and an agreement was worked out between *Comet* and the authors.

> But what an agreement! Out of $56.00 owed us, they offered two choices: 40% payable at once, without further claim, or the entire sum in six monthly installments .... Needing the money desperately, I persuaded Simak to agree to the former. Which meant my entire take for the story will be $11.00.[43]

VII

Jacobi's parents were growing old. Richard Jacobi had suffered heavily in the stock-market crash of 1929; and when he finally lost his job in 1938, his son inherited a serious financial responsibilty. Carl closed his office later that year, for he had become the family's sole breadwinner. "It's hell to be poor, all right," he complained to Derleth, "and it's just about time that my ship came in."[44]

He spent most of the next year working on a project which put his knowledge of the Far East to good use.

> I did some work for the Social Studies department of the Minneapolis Board of Education. I wrote and compiled *Paths to the Far East*, a thick volume about Malaysia, Indonesia, India, China, Burma, Tibet, and Baluchistan, which was used in the Minneapolis schools.[45]

While he looked for work after completing *Paths to the Far East*, Jacobi continued to write. "Sky Trap," an unremarkable novelette about the hijacking of a stratospheric airliner, which had been rejected by *Astounding Stories* in 1934, came out in *Science Fiction* (March, 1940); *Thrilling Mystery* published "Laughter in the Wind" (May, 1940), a weird-menace yarn set in North India and featuring an enormous striped hyena with drooling fangs; "Captain Jinx," a novelette concerning the fate of a deadly new explosive aboard a ship bound from Saigon to Kuching, was accepted by *Argosy* but appeared in its companion pulp, *Red Star Adventures* (August, 1940); *Weird Tales* ran "The Phantom Pistol" (May, 1941), a brooding tale of lycanthropy;[46] "The Street That Wasn't There," his collaboration with Clifford Simak about a professor of metaphysics who discovers that portions of the material world are mysteriously vanishing, came out in *Comet* (July, 1941); *Thrilling Adventures* published "Redemption Trail" (October, 1941), a story of pursuit through the Saputan head-hunting region of the North Borneo jungle; and "Hamadryad Chair" was rejected by *Thrilling Mystery*, but *10 Story Mystery Magazine* (February, 1942) ran this Borneo terror tale about a deadly wooden chair carved in the image of a writhing king cobra. By March, 1941, Jacobi was back to full-time fictioneering, but it didn't last. A month later he assumed editorship of *Midwest Media*, an advertising and radio trade journal.

> I wrote every stick of copy in the magazine except for a few feature articles. I interviewed prominent radio and advertising men in the Twin Cities; I wrote letters to prominent men in other cities in the midwest, and interviewed them by mail to be our "Man of the Month." I did a lot of leg work, getting pictures of billboards and radio personalities. I arranged to have cuts made

of these pictures and I made up the "dummy" of the magazine (with a little help but not much). In fact I might say that 90 percent of all copy in the magazine was mine. Writing headlines for each article and deciding on the style of typeface was also part of my duties.[47]

It was good experience, but the salary, he grumbled, "would insult a filing clerk."[48] He wasn't vexed for long. In September, *Midwest Media* reorganized, took on a municipal liquor publication, and its editor assumed Jacobi's position. After only four months with the firm, Jacobi was out of a job. A few weeks later, he described his plight:

I've been dividing my time, combing the city for other employment and trying to grind out saleable copy. Unfortunately financial worries do not make for a clear writing brain, and I'm working under difficulty, stalling off creditors.[49]

He eventually landed a short-term appointment.

For a brief period I returned to the University of Minnesota campus, where I helped manage what was called the Key Center of War Information. This was so-called publicity, but don't let the name fool you. Actually it was a propaganda bureau, highly regarded in those days of mad patriotism. I did a lot of PR work, wrote radio sketches, and arranged to have various professors write speeches praising the war effort. You'd be surprised at some of the inane, grammatically incorrect texts I had to rewrite to make presentable.[50]

The Minneapolis Fantasy Society continued to meet at the YMCA and elswhere (Jacobi hosted one meeting at his lake cabin on 23 May 1941), but America's entry into the Second World War quickly depleted its ranks. Doug Blakely, Rodman Allen and John Chapman were the first to be drafted, followed soon thereafter by Donald Wandrei, who later served with General George S. Patton's Third Army during the invasion of the Rhineland; National Defense nabbed Oliver Saari, and Clifford Simak accepted a position with Army Intelligence. It seemed likely that the MFS would be forced to disband; but at the last minute, Sam Russell and Morrie Dollens were deferred, and the group remained active throughout the Forties.[51]

Because of his parents' dependency and his father's heart condition, Carl Jacobi was considered a hardship case and was not inducted. Convinced that he couldn't sell enough fiction to keep his

head above water, he went to work on 25 September 1942 at the
Honeywell defense plant (where Oliver Saari had been employed on
the night shift for the past year). He put in eight hours a day, seven
days a week, and worried constantly because he was neglecting the
typewriter.

> ...as an electronics inspector I was very much a fish out of
> water.
> ...I had to learn to read and operate some very delicate gauges
> and devices, but I wasn't good at it, for the simple reason that the
> work didn't interest me.[52]
> I didn't know what a micrometer was, let alone know how to read
> one. And a turret lathe and a drill press were simply devices that
> made a lot of noise, as far as I was concerned.[53]

Even for an inspector, it was "man-killing work,"[54] and by 1945
Jacobi had developed a mild case of neurasthenia. "My whole
physical makeup screams at working in a factory," he told Derleth,
"but my hands are tied, since I'm the sole support of the family."[55]
The years snailed by, his parents grew more dependent (Richard
turned 73 in 1945, Matie 69), and Jacobi's Honeywell service wound
up consuming twenty-three years.

Whenever he found a scrap of free time, Jacobi returned
faithfully to his writing desk. "After a day at the plant," he wrote, "I
find myself so exhausted it's difficult to do even the shortest spell at
the typewriter."[56] Yet he persisted, night after night, and managed
to keep writing, rewriting, and selling. Although he had never been
particularly devoted to the field of science fiction, and preferred to
work in the genre of the macabre, Jacobi realized that the Forties
were an era of comparative prosperity for science-fiction literature;
needing the financial returns that this type of fiction brought in, he
began to turn out science-fiction stories with more creative energy
than at any other point in his career. His success in marketing them
was immediate, for Malcolm Reiss, general manager of *Planet
Stories*, purchased six in quick succession. The "Cosmic Castaway"
(March, 1943) is an interplanetary buccaneer who raids the space
lanes to vanquish the villainous Sirians, in a grandiose novelette
inspired by Sabatini and originally entitled "The Space Hawk." In
"Assignment on Venus" (Fall, 1943), an Earthman threatened with
dishonorable discharge from the Venusian colonial service for
refusing to obey orders foils a scheme to loot priceless rejuvenating
crystals by preventing a war between two native tribes; if this
sounds familiar, it's because Jacobi simply restirred motifs from a

1934 adventure yarn, "Letter of Dismissal," and transferred the plot
from Borneo to Venus. Elderly science-fiction writer Annabella C.
Flowers, better known as Grannie Annie, an outrageous character
who drinks whiskey and swears like a pirate, thwarts a Venusian
villain's bid for galactic dictatorship in the wildly improbable
"Doctor Universe" (Fall, 1944).[57] The delightful crackpot returns in
"Double Trouble" (Spring, 1945), as Grannie Annie combats Red
Spot Fever on Jupiter—an even sillier story than its predecessor. In
"Enter the Nebula" (Fall, 1946), the greatest cracksman in the
galaxy avenges the murder of his father in a desperate attempt to
save Mars from annihilation; reminiscent of the Jimmie Dale yarns
of Frank L. Packard, the novelette also resembles E. W. Hornung's
adventures of gentleman thief A. J. Raffles (as well as Jacobi's own
stories about Stephen Benedict), and is a good example of straight
adventure converted, detail for detail, into science fiction. A sequel,
"The Nebula and the Necklace," written in 1945, never sold.[58]
Jacobi's final appearance in *Planet Stories* was his finest:
"Tepondicon" (Winter, 1946), in which an adventurer visits the
seven plague-ridden cities of Jupiter's High Ganymedian Plateau in
search of a fabulous stone of immense power. To reach it, he must
pass through one of two portals: one leads to the Jupiter Stone; the
other, to death. The closing line is a gem: "Of course, you all know
which door I opened."[59] Jacobi still rates "Tepondicon" highly; its
"lady-or-the-tiger ending," he maintains, makes it one of the best
science-fiction pieces he's ever produced. Three more yarns were
accepted by Leo Margulies for *Startling Stories*. One of exceptional
merit is "Canal," which Lurton Blassingame, one of Jacobi's
literary agents, had submitted to *Astounding Science-Fiction*; when
editor John W. Campbell, Jr., turned it down, Margulies bought it
and ran it in *Startling Stories* (Spring, 1944).[60] This tale of high
adventure on Mars (a reworking of his 1935 "Quarry") concerns the
pursuit of an Earthman through a labyrinthine chasm of
desolation, and the other-dimensional space warp into which he
stumbles. "The Cosmic Doodler" (Fall, 1944), rejected earlier (under
its original title, "Space Scribblers") by Campbell's *Astounding
Science-Fiction* and Hugo Gernsback's *Amazing Stories,* tells of a
psychology professor who receives an ominous warning from
another world, across thousands of light years of space, through
cosmic telepathy. In "Lodana" (September, 1947), treacherous
mutant workers revolt against their Earth masters; the result of
widely separated periods of writing, it was a minor effort, but earned
Jacobi 1½¢ per word, a better rate than he'd been getting for some
time.

Weird Tales was still one of Jacobi's most lucrative markets. Its editor, since Farnsworth Wright's retirement and subsequent death in 1940, was Dorothy McIlwraith, who would remain with the magazine until its demise in 1954. McIlwraith, who also published Jacobi's adventure yarns in *Weird Tales'* companion pulp, *Short Stories*, was initially unimpressed by the first "weird" he had written during the war years, and rejected it in 1943; but after he revised it according to August Derleth's suggestions in 1944, McIlwraith bought it for *Weird Tales*.[61] So Jacobi was back, with "Carnaby's Fish" (July, 1945), an exquisitely beautiful mermaid.

Jacobi captured the swashbuckling glamour of a more colorful age in "Black Lace" (*Thrilling Adventures*, November, 1943), a buccaneering tale of the Spanish Main. Rapiers clash as daring freebooter Steven Lace joins forces with his fellow "Brethren of the Coast" to fight the oppression of the Spanish *conquistadores* in 1675. Although Jacobi's English fencing master-turned-pirate was modeled along the lines of Rafael Sabatini's Captain Blood, the novelette, curiously enough, was originally written as a "weird" in 1938; when Lurton Blassingame failed to sell it to either *Weird Tales* or *Strange Stories*, Jacobi rewrote it as a straight adventure yarn in 1941—a fortunate transformation indeed, for it is one of the most skillful pieces of adventure fiction he's ever written.

Another action story which Jacobi wrote during this period was a Borneo adventure entitled "Submarine I-26." Following rejections from Rogers Terrill at *Argosy* and Dorothy McIlwraith of *Short Stories*, it was featured in the March, 1944, issue of *Doc Savage*. Modern war stories made timely yarns and were much in demand in the early Forties, for interest in the Far East was high, but acquiring current background information was particularly ticklish. All of Jacobi's old locales, which he knew so well from years of correspondence and research, including Samarinda, Singapore, Tandjong-Selor, Kuching, Makassar, Bandjermasin, and Palembang, had by now been overrun by the Japanese. Should he write in blissful disregard of all recent war developments, giving readers the impression that the action had taken place some time in the immediate past, thereby running the risk of editorial rejection because the tale was too dated? On the other hand, were he to write a contemporary war story, which would require more meticulous planning, the yarn might be outdated by the time it reached an editor's hands. Jacobi chose the latter course, and wrote to Arthur Leo Zagat of the Writers' War Board for assistance. Zagat contacted the Department of Naval Intelligence and arranged for Jacobi to obtain government background material on Japanese subs. "Submarine I-26" concerns the thirty men stationed at the Borneo outpost of Long Nawang (with whose commanding officer Jacobi had corresponded), and their escape from the Japanese-held island aboard a captured enemy sub.

> This part of the story required an intimate knowledge of submarines, and I spent a devil of a lot of time on research. Lucky enough to get the styles, dimensions and names of Japanese undersea boats as of immediately before Pearl Harbor. What interested me, however, was this: I believe Jules Verne's story, *Twenty Thousand Leagues Under the Sea*, was written around 1875, long before any practical undersea boat had been built. Yet the dimensions, the length, the width, and the inner machinery of the craft he describes are almost identical to the large U-boats now in operation. Curious, isn't it.[62]

Encouraged by the success of the 1943 motion picture *Destination Tokyo*, which starred Cary Grant as the commander of an American sub sent into Japanese waters, Jacobi was confident that "Submarine I-26" had screen possibilities, and sent the story to his Hollywood agent. The studios, however, weren't interested. Later in 1944, Carl tried his hand at another medium: radio scripts. Pulp writer Nelson S. Bond (1908-   ) of Roanoke, Virginia, anxious to devote more time to magazine work, asked him to ghostwrite an episode of his radio series, *Hot Copy*, which was broadcast every Sunday over the Blue network. Jacobi dropped everything and quickly fired off "The Case of the Ten Dollar Bill," a provocative tale about counterfeiting, but it was never aired. He also considered writing copy for the *First Nighter* program and NBC sportscaster Bill Stern, but, reluctant to let his pulp work slide, he soon abandoned that idea.

When the war had finally run its course in 1945, Carl Jacobi had just turned 37. His eyes were brown, his hair black; he stood nearly five feet eleven inches tall, weighed 160 pounds and was not ill-favored in looks. Yet he hadn't married. The reason was as simple as it was laudable: filial piety. His attention to his parents' physical needs, which necessitated his staying reasonably close to home, prevented him in large measure from seeking a suitable partner in marriage. The closest he ever came to taking the big step was, he joked years later, when he served as best man at Harry and Lois Blade's wedding on 20 August 1938—"And then I damn near lost the ring."[63] Although he dated frequently through the years, he has remained a lifelong bachelor. He recalls an amusing incident which took place in the mid-Forties:

> ... in those days my circle of acquaintances included one
> attractive girl who was devoted to dancing, and since this form
> of entertainment was not my long suit she insisted I take some
> lessons. Accordingly, with reluctance, I called at a local studio.
> The lone attendant was busy, so I lit my pipe and waited. Five
> minutes later, when she was free, I knocked the ashes from my
> pipe out the window and was presently engaged in the
> intricacies of the latest dance step. Abruptly I heard sounds of
> confusion outside. And then a helmeted fireman burst in the
> room and demanded to know who had been smoking cigarettes.
> With a perfectly blank face I assured him I never smoked
> cigarettes. After he had gone I looked out the window. In the
> street below were several fire rigs and a network of hoses. And I
> saw with horror that the whole damned awning of the shop
> below was consumed by flames.[64]

Jacobi was paid a fine compliment in October, 1945, when the
program director of the University of Minnesota's Extension
Division wrote him that he had proposed a course in Pulp Story
Writing Methods, and had recommended Jacobi as its instructor. He
had sent similar letters to members of the English faculty,
suggesting that Jacobi be considered for the position. Carl
enthusiastically submitted a prospectus, and had several young
professors pulling for him, but Joseph Warren Beach, conservative
chairman of the English Department, while admitting that Jacobi's
outline was a scholarly piece of work, didn't deem the course suitable
college material, and it was never offered.

VIII

In July, 1944, Jacobi had written Derleth to inquire whether
Arkham House was devoted solely to fantasy fiction, or whether the
firm might be interested in bringing out a collection of his Borneo
adventure tales. The stories Jacobi specifically had in mind were
"Hamadryad Chair," "Smoke of the Snake," "Letter of Dismissal,"
"East of Samarinda," "Quarry," "Dead Man's River," "Jungle
Wires," "Spider Wires," "Death's Outpost," "Deceit Post," "A Film
in the Bush," "Leopard Tracks," "Sumpitan," "Submarine I-26,"
"Satan's Kite," "Crocodile," and "Trial by Jungle." Many of these,
he pointed out, had a weird angle, and some were straight "weirds"
written with logical resolutions; all were carefully researched, and
could be supplemented with several sea stories set in the
surrounding East Indian waters, including "Holt Sails the 'San

Hing'," "Heliotrope Cruise" ("Captain Jinx"), and "Black Passage." Derleth was unenthusiastic, but later proposed, in November, 1944, that Arkham House publish a collection of Jacobi's best work in the domain of the uncanny. Within a few days, Jacobi sent Derleth a letter (dated 11 November 1944) which suggested the stories he wanted in the book. It is a revealing letter, for it mentions many tales that were not eventually included in the collection: "Smoke of the Snake," "Hamadryad Chair," "Death's Outpost," "Head in His Hands," "Laughter in the Wind," and "Murder for Medusa"; a few unpublished yarns ("Woman of the Witch-Flowers," "Hall of the Devil-Flag," and "Bride of the Tree-Men"); and several pieces which came out in subsequent Arkham House collections ("The War of the Weeds" and two that he had recently completed, "The Random Quantity" and "Tepondicon"). While Derleth was procuring the reprint rights in 1945, Jacobi got to work tightening the stories, restoring original titles, and, in a few instances, supplying new titles. In August, 1945, he told Derleth:

> I have gone through several of the stories, cutting out an unnecessary word here or there and eliminating several paragraphs you mentioned. In "The Coach on the Ring" I chopped out the second paragraph entirely; it was put in by the editor.[65]
> ...I cut "The Satanic Piano" more than a thousand words—all chaff, and I sliced liberally from the overwritten conclusion of "Revelations in Black" and "The Tomb from Beyond."[66]

Revelations in Black appeared in 1947; a collection of pulse-quickeners to be savored best on dark, lonely, stormy nights, it contained many of Jacobi's finest tales of terror and the supernatural: "Phantom Brass," "The Cane," "The Coach on the Ring" ("The Haunted Ring"), "The Kite" ("Satan's Kite"), "Canal," "The Satanic Piano," "The Last Drive," "The Spectral Pistol" ("The Phantom Pistol"), "Sagasta's Last," "The Tomb from Beyond," "The Digging at Pistol Key," "Moss Island," "Carnaby's Fish," "The King and the Knave" ("The Devil Deals"), "Cosmic Teletype," "A Pair of Swords," "A Study in Darkness" ("Spawn of Blackness"), "Mive," "Writing on the Wall" ("The Cosmic Doodler"), "The Face in the Wind" and the title story, "Revelations in Black." Fellow fictioneeer Robert Bloch (1917-) accorded it a glowing review in the Winter, 1948, issue of *The Arkham Sampler*:

> Carl Jacobi's concept is, at first glance, the velvet pall, the midnight moor, the unlit house, the *mysterioso* chord on the piano—in a word, the conventional, almost traditional "stage

effect" or backdrop for the saga of the supernatural. It is the inevitable background for the mysterious veiled woman in "Revelations in Black," the genius recently released from the asylum in "The Satanic Piano," and the diabolical stranger of "The Coach on the Ring." Yet one cannot dismiss the Jacobi gambit quite this easily. On the surface, his use of "black" is proper to the atmosphere of "manors" and "lodgings" and "laboratories" so familiar to readers of the standard weird tale. But on closer examination of thematic material, one notes the peculiar correspondence of darkness in the background and mental disorder in the characters who emerge from that background.

Another dark thread in the Jacobi pattern is the "demoniac possession" which menaces his characters. It would seem then, that to Carl Jacobi, "black" symbolizes the mental blackout of insanity.

Let no one despair that the "good old days" of fantastic fiction are past. As long as writers like Bradbury, Jacobi and Leiber can consistently produce stories of this calibre, the future of the weird tale is far from dark.[67]

Ten of Jacobi's most effective chillers had appeared in *Weird Tales* since 1932. Eight more ran between 1947 and 1950. Swathed in gloom and limned against a gray-black sky, a Gothic manor house provides the backdrop for an array of cowled figures, wooded glades and grisly pagan sacrifices which await those who pass through "The Corbie Door" (May, 1947); August Derleth's criticisms had been helpful early on, and he later encouraged Lamont Buchanan, associate editor of *Weird Tales*, to publish the novelette. "The Digging at Pistol Key" (July, 1947), which also profited from Derleth's comments, is an equally gruesome yarn set in Trinidad, involving obeah worship, buried pirate treasure, murder, retribution, and an ominous, shallow grave. In Port-of-Spain, Trinidad, a voodoo curse hangs over a "Portrait in Moonlight" (November, 1947); like the man in the picture, its youth-obsessed owner is gradually growing younger. With mounting horror, he fears his imminent regression beyond infancy into oblivion. Reminiscent of Oscar Wilde's *The Picture of Dorian Gray*, "Portrait in Moonlight" was the title story of Jacobi's second Arkham House collection in 1964.

In "The Lorenzo Watch" (January, 1948), revised according to Derleth's recommendations but rejected by Donald A. Wollheim for his *Avon Fantasy Reader* series, a gentleman with a singular knack for locating things that other persons have lost arranges his nagging wife's death by drowning; after the "accident," he begins to notice the ticking—that incessant, maddening ticking of the watch she had always worn—and the body cannot be found in its watery grave. Variable channels of time and space are explored in "The La Prello Paper" (March, 1948), a Jacobi classic which relates how an old-fashioned gentleman who lives in the past steps through a beckoning billboard sign into a fourth-dimensional world of horse-drawn vehicles, watering troughs, and hitching posts. As if pursued by some demon, a ghostly white stallion approaches the brink of a cliff at full gallop, hesitates but an instant, then plunges into the sea with its female rider, in "Incident at the Galloping Horse" (November, 1948); set amid the ruins of a seventeenth-century tavern on Tortola in the British Virgin Islands, this atmospheric West Indian tale evokes memories of "The Coach on the Ring" and remains one of its author's personal favorites. Some of Jacobi's most inspired plotting is found in "Matthew South and Company" (May, 1949), a tightly woven study of frenzied obsession and murder which handles the *Doppelganger* motif with considerable invention: a mill owner in Port-of-Spain, Trinidad, who harbors a profound aversion to his own name, hides behind a variety of fanciful pseudonyms (including several of Jacobi's own: James K. Vermont, Philip Spayne and Matthew South)—a harmless little eccentricity, until he's confronted by three mysterious strangers (alter egos all) who claim to be Vermont, Spayne and South. "The Spanish Camera" (September, 1950) is without equal: not only does its fogged lens record indistinct images of subjects which are hundreds of miles distant, but it has also begun to commit murder. Suggestive of "Sagasta's Last," the yarn marked Jacobi's final appearance in "The Unique Magazine" before it ceased publication in 1954.

After receiving rejections from *Ellery Queen's Mystery Magazine, Weird Tales* and *Esquire*, Jacobi sold "The Random Quantity" for the fairly high rate of 2¢ per word to Donald A. Wollheim, who brought it out in the new digest-sized magazine, the *Avon Fantasy Reader No. 5*, in 1947. The story reveals what was dreadfully wrong with the Mowbilay print that adorned the laboratory wall—the one depicting the gambling casino, the roulette wheel and the blonde with the smoking derringer. With its unexpected ending and an adroitly handled flashback within a flashback, Jacobi's tale of the fabulous carving known as "The Jade Scarlotti" (*Short Stories*, July 10, 1948) is one Borneo adventure that, together with "Smoke of the Snake" and "Crocodile," should have been anthologized years ago. A salvage depot on a barren asteroid is the setting for "Gentlemen, the Scavengers!" (*Thrilling Wonder Stories*, April, 1948), a melodramatic science-fiction yarn about an attempt to preserve the interplanetary balance of power. More successful was "The Historian" (*Startling Stories*, May, 1950), a delightfully humorous short-short which lampooned science-fiction pulps. In it, Jacobi tells why a famed Martian scholar of the distant future committed suicide on the eve of completing a monumental, definitive history of the solar system: he had gone mad after reading newly discovered documents which invalidated every fact, date and event he had ever chronicled. And the nature of these documents? "They were of a peculiar type made in twentieth-century Earth with bright colored covers. They were known as magazines ... *science-fiction magazines.*"[68]

Despite his success with science fiction, Jacobi felt constrained to confess to Derleth that he was quickly losing whatever interest he had in writing that type of story. In December, 1949, he wrote: "...I've taken a dislike—this is confidential—for the entire SF field."[69] In January, 1950:

> I'll tell you why I'm down on science fiction. It's because of the Campbell influence, which has taken out all the warmth and left a cold type of narrative about as colorless as a deep-freeze unit.[70]

And again in May, 1954:

> It may be strange for an SF writer to say it, but I enjoy very little of the SF I read. Some of the modern writing seems sophomoric to me.[71]

This didn't prevent him, however, from joining the Science Fiction Writers of America in 1966, after noting that Ray Bradbury and August Derleth, among prominent others, were active members.

In 1948, Jacobi produced "Her Impulse Day," a romance aimed at the slicks. After *Ladies' Home Journal* turned it down, the yarn sold for 6¢ a word to Toronto's *Star Weekly* (May 21, 1949). It was reprinted in the *New Zealand Woman's Weekly* (July 21, 1949), and also appeared in translation in Montreal's French-language newspaper, *La Patrie* (27 August 1949). Jacobi later observed:

> It must pay to write boy-girl romance. Including reprints and even deducting fifteen percent Canadian copyright fees, that story has brought in to date more money than anything I've written.[72]

Another "slick" attempt, "Love's Sweet Name," misfired and bounced at both *Today's Woman* and *Ladies' Home Journal* in 1951. "The Kid from Harmony," a story about a swing orchestra, almost made it at every magazine to which it was submitted, but never quite sold. Aimed at *The Saturday Evening Post*, it was begun during the war, completed in 1947, and passed through the editorial offices of *The American, Collier's, The Saturday Evening Post, Argosy, This Week, The Blue Book Magazine, Ladies' Home Journal* and *Liberty* before Jacobi gave up on it in 1949. He considered it a high compliment that all but two of these magazines sent him personal letters of refusal; as they customarily received hundreds of submissions per month, it was standard practice to use rejection slips. "Grandmother's Writing Desk," written in 1949, was similarly first-class "slick" material, but it missed the mark at *Ladies' Home Journal, Today's Woman, Cosmopolitan, Woman's Home Companion* and Toronto's *Star Weekly*. Jacobi rewrote it as "The Secret Compartment" in 1958, but that too failed to sell. One of the few Jacobi "weirds" that never made it was "Josephine Gage," a 1947 voodoo tale set in Port-of-Spain, Trinidad. *Weird Tales* accepted the story in October of that year, but at the last minute rejected it in favor of "The La Prello Paper," which had been submitted at the same time. Jacobi believes that Dorothy McIlwraith would have used "Josephine Gage" if she hadn't had the two yarns from which to choose. He sent in a revised version of the story in 1949, but this time McIlwraith bounced it for good.

IX

A colorful era was passing from the scene. The fact that Jacobi had started to concentrate more on "slick" work was a clear indication that all was not well with the pulps. A wartime paper shortage had redirected much of the available wood pulp into the new paperback industry, and inexpensive paperbacks had been steadily undermining pulp sales since the end of the war. By the early Fifties, many of the old standbys had already gone under, and those which had managed to hang on found the going rough. Declining readership and constant financial crises led to retrenchment and cost cutting, most evident in the increasing use of reprint material; even such stalwarts as *Weird Tales* (issued bi-monthly since January, 1940), *Short Stories* and *Adventure* were forced to resort to reprinting stories, excellent though they were. In an effort to give the paperback market a run for its money, some of the surviving pulps abandoned the old 7″ x 10″ format in favor of the 5½″ x 8″ digest size, which Campbell's *Astounding* had inaugurated in November, 1943. Nothing helped. Sales continued to drop, and the day of reckoning was at hand. *Weird Tales*, which had adopted the smaller digest size in September, 1953, folded in September, 1954, after publishing its 279th issue. *Startling Stories, Planet Stories* and *Thrilling Wonder Stories* gave up their respective ghosts in 1955; the list of casualties is as long as it is disheartening. Jacobi has always maintained that converting to digest size worked against the pulps, for readers simply didn't feel they were getting their money's worth; the larger pulp format, he insists, would have given the magazines better display on the newsstands, and hence a better chance for recovery.

His letters to Derleth from this point on fairly bristle with references to dwindling markets. In March, 1956, he wrote:

> With *Weird Tales* gone and all the adventure magazines given way to the men's-true-fact-sex magazines and the SF market faltering, I feel like a fish out of water. I simply don't know what to write or whom to write for. In the past I've always had a potential market.[73]

In November, 1960:

> ... I believe I could be selling regularly today if all my markets had not collapsed, leaving me high and dry. There's not an editor in the field who knows me except perhaps Leo Margulies, and he has only one magazine left.[74]

Again in June, 1961:

> Is there no market for what formerly was referred to as pulp fiction? The weird magazines are no more; the science-fiction magazines have dwindled; *Amazing* and *Fantastic* have reverted to reprints. I don't know of a single publication devoted to the adventure story without a heavy emphasis on the sex angle or an even heavier emphasis on the true-fact article. Yet I remember when *Adventure* appeared semi-monthly and *Argosy* was a weekly best seller. How times have changed.[75]

And again in March, 1962:

> Time was when the weekly mail would bring a request from a magazine, new or old, for material, or at least the

Carl (early 1950s)

Carl (21 March 1954)

announcement of a new publication. Not any more. All the
magazines I used to write for have dropped by the wayside, and I
certainly feel cut off. Nor can I get excited over the new crop of
science fiction that is slowly dwindling on the stands. The
golden age of the pulps has given way to the sex mishmash of the
paperback, and not for the better, I might add.[76]

Nevertheless, there remained an audience for fantasy fiction,
and with the passing of the pulps came a handful of new digest-sized
publications which partially filled the void: *The Magazine of
Fantasy and Science Fiction* made its debut in October, 1949,
followed by *Galaxy Magazine* and *Imagination* in October, 1950, *If*
(March, 1952), *Fantastic* (Summer, 1952), and *Fantastic Universe*
(June-July, 1953), to name but a few. Although markets for short
fiction were now limited, Jacobi and other members of the
fictioneering fraternity were back in business.

Scott Meredith, Jacobi's new literary agent, sold three tales to
Leo Margulies, publisher and editorial director of *Fantastic
Universe*. After extensive rewriting suggested by August Derleth,
"The Tanganyika TV" appeared as "Made in Tanganyika" (May,
1954); this necromantic fantasy concerns a conchologist's curious
television set and an alien expanse of beach littered with
unclassifiable shells. In "Strangers to Straba" (October, 1954), a
derelict spaceship thunders across a lonely planet with an appalling
fixation of purpose, "like a monster of metal gone mad."[77] An
exploratory expedition from Earth journeys far into the future in
another science-fiction yarn, "The Long Voyage" (September, 1955),
an old reject from 1948 which had been turned down by *Thrilling
Wonder Stories, Planet Stories*, and *Super-Science Fiction*.

"Witches in the Cornfield" is perhaps Jacobi's most memorable
story from the Fifties: was it their imagination, or did the children
really see that scarecrow descend from its pole, kick up its heels, and
begin to dance in the moonlight? A ghastly tale of voodoo vengeance
and decapitation, it was published as "The Dangerous Scarecrow"
in the August, 1954, issue of *Imagination*; in an accompanying
autobiographical sketch, Jacobi discussed the story's origins:

> "The Dangerous Scarecrow" grew out of a double example of
> fast-disappearing Americana which I sighted from a southern
> Minnesota road—two scarecrows facing each other across
> adjacent fields, remarkably well clothed.[78]

"The Legation Cigar," featuring Jo Domingo, the "island

detective" with the Trinidad Constabulary, was an old short which hadn't made the grade at *Ellery Queen's Mystery Magazine* in 1948. After Jacobi reworked it in 1956, Scott Meredith sold the tale to *The Saint Detective Magazine* (August, 1957); it was reprinted in the August, 1958, British edition of the same magazine, and resurfaced again in *The Saint Mystery Library*, a 1959 paperback. Meredith also placed "The Martian Calendar" with *Space Science Fiction Magazine* (Spring, 1957); in it, a cyclical time warp leads to reenactments of a brutal murder—again and again and again. Two science-fiction yarns first saw print in hardbound anthologies edited by August Derleth. A colonial official stationed on Venus tries to destroy the electronic brain of his new assistant, a quick-witted robot, in "The Gentleman Is an Epwa," which came out in *Worlds of Tomorrow* (1953); the story was reprinted in the November, 1953, issue of *Cosmos Science Fiction and Fantasy*. Horrors beset explorers on planet Renit-4, as they encounter the guardians of "The White Pinnacle," featured in the 1954 anthology, *Time To Come*.

X

One of the biggest headaches which plagued all pulp writers was the length of time it frequently took to guide a story into print. With meticulous craftsmen like Carl Jacobi, a manuscript was ready for submission only after endless hours of pruning and polishing. Yet for every yarn that sold on its first trip out, three or four would invariably develop India-rubber tendencies. As most writers preferred checks to rejection slips, it was often necessary to rebuild a tale from scratch, with no assurance of landing a sale. Eventually either the story would be placed or the discouraged author would abandon his efforts to peddle it. One science-fiction yarn that Jacobi gave up on, "The Brothers Dalfay," was a fiasco from the start. It had defied completion when he first wrote it in 1954; a revised version was turned down by *Fantastic Universe* in 1956; and, although he rewrote the story in 1957, it never sold. "The Commission of Captain Lace" did, but only after years of frustration. A sequel to the swashbuckler "Black Lace," it was penned with the title "A Letter of Marque" toward the close of 1943, just as Jacobi's buccaneer hero was making his debut in the November, 1943, issue of *Thrilling Adventures*. Jacobi considered it one of the most polished shorts he'd ever produced, but editors disagreed. Agent Lurton Blassingame returned it after trying all available markets, and Jacobi's high hopes were dashed after *Maclean's Magazine* in Toronto and *The Blue Book Magazine* rejected it as well. In 1948, he rewrote it as "The Commission of Captain Lace," but it failed to click with *Adventure, The Blue Book Magazine, Short Stories* or Toronto's *Star Weekly*. After agent Scott Meredith turned it down as unmarketable in 1956, Jacobi sent it off to the revived *Short Stories Magazine*, which was back on the newsstands with a new publisher (Leo Margulies), editor (Cylvia Kleinman) and format (digest size). Kleinman bounced it after holding the mansucript more than six months, but took it a year later. Rapiers flashed again in the Caribbean, when "The Commission of Captain Lace" finally saw print in the April, 1958, issue of *Short Stories Magazine*. "The La Prello Paper," in welcome contrast, met with no difficulties. Jacobi completed it in September, 1947, received an acceptance from *Weird Tales* in October and was informed in December that the story would appear in the March, 1948, 25th-anniversary issue of the magazine, as indeed it did.

XI

Although Carl Jacobi, unlike many pulp writers, has technically never used a nom de plume, he has toyed with pseudonyms most of his life. "As a by-line I've always disliked my name," he admitted in 1977. "To me it sounded harsh and not at all euphonious."[79] As a youngster, he considered using Decatur De Koven, the nickname his father had given him, and soon began to fashion an array of fanciful pen names, including James K. Vermont, Philip Spayne, Matthew South, King Marling, Jay Colby, Jefferson Crewe, Christopher Weed, Reynard Fox, Richard East, Richard Carle, Carl Richards, Charles Richards and Carlos Ricardo. But his favorite—both as a by-line and as a character—has always been Stephen Benedict. The names Ethan South and Stephen Benedict adorn the flyleaf of one of Carl's junior high textbooks, and one of his university texts is similarly inscribed: "Property of the famous Stephen Benedict." As a gentleman burglar, Benedict figures in "Rumbling Cannon," Jacobi's first appearance in a professional magazine, and in three stories published in the *Minnesota Quarterly* ("The Borgian Chandelier," "Enter Stephen Benedict" and "The Masked Orange"); he turns up again as a detective in "Satan's Roadhouse." Stephen Benedict came early and stayed late: to this day, Jacobi's calling card bears Benedict's name under his own. Ironically, the only time a Jacobi story appeared under a pseudonym, the by-line was not of his own choosing. The January, 1937, *Thrilling Adventures* ran two Jacobi yarns: "Dead Man's River" and "Spider Wires." As the Thrilling Publication pulps customarily employed a "house name"whenever more than one story by the same author was published in a single issue, "Spider Wires" was attributed to Jackson Cole.

Throughout the years, Jacobi has received his share of letters from over-enthusiastic fans, as well as from those only too willing to share their expertise in arcane matters.

> ... I was rather taken by the introductory paragraph to "Smoke of the Snake," and so apparently was a reader. That opening passage read: "Herrick arrived in Samarinda at night when it was late enough for him to slip unnoticed by the strict and watchful Dutch immigration authorities and sufficiently dark to remove all chances of detection by the native police."
>
> Shortly after that weird story was published in Street & Smith's *Top-Notch* magazine, I received an unsigned postcard from California. It read: "Henderson arrived in San Diego when it was late enough for him to slip unnoticed by the strict and watchful room clerk and sufficiently dark to remove all chances of detection by the house detective."
>
> Thereafter, at intervals of a week or so, I received similar cards from Panama, Lisbon, Alexandria, Bombay, Bangkok, Singapore, etc. Some chap with a sense of humor and a penchant for story "beginnings" was apparently on a world cruise and postcarded me along the way. The final card read: "Henderson arrived back home when it was late enough for him to go to bed and sufficiently dark to remove any chances of a good night's sleep."
>
> Another story, "Satan's Roadhouse," prompted a reader to write. In the tale I had occasion to mention a python, and I referred to it as cold and slimy to the touch. Some chap who operated a snake farm in Louisiana wrote to say that a snake's skin is dry and hard. Which is true, of course. Being hard pressed for an answer, I replied that my particular python had been treated with a chemical solution which I had neglected to mention in the story. It wasn't very good, but it was all I could think of. I felt a little sheepish when he wrote back and apologized.[80]

In the spring of 1955 Standard Magazines wrote Jacobi that his 1937 Borneo adventure tale, "Dead Man's River," had received a tentative offer of $250 for TV adaptation, and asked that he release residual rights to them so they could market the story on a fifty-fifty basis. When August Derleth advised that a fifty-percent publisher's take was rather steep for television rights, Jacobi requested that Standard improve its original offer. This brought a terse reply: if and when the Hollywood deal went through, they would do the right thing. Jacobi heard nothing for months, and assumed it had fallen through. It had. Nearly a year later, Standard Magazines informed him that another Borneo story had been selected. This remains Jacobi's only television offer to date. An earlier overture from Hollywood, concerning a possible radio broadcast of "The Cane" in 1946, had been even less encouraging. Jacobi's potential take? No cash, but plenty of exposure and free publicity. He turned it down flat.

XII

Richard Jacobi passed away on 4 March 1955, at the age of 82. He had been in failing health for years. His son suddenly found life rather meaningless and futile, and shared his sorrow with August Derleth:

> Of course 82 is considered a long life span, I suppose, but living at home as I do, I was closer to my dad than most sons my age, and there's going to be a void that will be hard to forget. Up until the last year when he took to his bed, we spent many an evening hour discussing books, music and his favorite pastime, history .... That leaves just three Jacobis left: myself, my mother, and my aunt.[81]
> At best, I'm a poor chip off the old block. Dad was much more of an extrovert; even in his late seventies he was full of personality and was a well-read man. He knew music and the theater, had boxes of old-time programs and some forty full-score operas which he loved to play on the piano.[82]

Jacobi's second collection of fantasy tales for Arkham House had been in the planning stages since 1953. Originally scheduled for inclusion were "Kincaid's Car," "The White Pinnacle" and "Gentlemen, The Scavengers," three science-fiction yarns which subsequently appeared in his third effort for Arkham House in 1972. Once again Jacobi restored original titles and edited some of the stories. In June, 1962, he wrote Derleth:

> Following your suggestion, I've been getting together the magazines containing the stories for *Portraits in Moonlight*, compressing the wordage, smoothing over rough spots; in some cases the selections were hard to make, one for another; but I

believe I've a fair representation. Some of the titles in your catalogue listing were never written, of course.[83]

And again the following month:

> In reading for corrections the typescript of *Portraits in Moonlight*, I found five pages of the title story heavy with overwriting which for some unknown reason I had passed in published form. It was necessary to delete one page entirely and to cross out whole paragraphs and sentences on the other four (no additions or corrections, however).
>
> If it were just a matter of these five pages I wouldn't concern myself, but I would like to cut some from "The Corbie Door" also, and possibly from others.[84]

Portraits in Moonlight was finally published in 1964. Besides the title story, "Portrait in Moonlight," it contained "The Martian Calendar," "The Corbie Door," "Tepondicon," "Made in Tanganyika," "Long Voyage" ("The Long Voyage"), "The Historian," "Lodana," "The Lorenzo Watch," "The Spanish Camera" and four of Jacobi's most haunting tales of the supernatural: "Matthew South and Company," "The La Prello Paper," "Incident at the Galloping Horse," and "Witches in the Cornfield" ("The Dangerous Scarecrow"). He dedicated the book to the memory of his father. It was well received, and Robert A. W. Lowndes recommended it with enthusiasm in an August, 1965, *Magazine of Horror* review.

Many fantasists—Clark Ashton Smith, Robert E. Howard, Frank Belknap Long, August Derleth, Robert Bloch, Henry Kuttner, Colin Wilson, J. Ramsey Campbell, and Brian Lumley, among others—have written stories incorporating elements from H. P. Lovecraft's Cthulhu tales concerning a race of creatures that ruled the Earth eons ago, were driven out, and from their distant abode, await the moment of their return to power. Although several of Carl Jacobi's stories (most notably "The Tomb from Beyond" and "The Corbie Door") bear the imprint of Lovecraft's influence, Jacobi produced but one Cthulhu yarn: "The Aquarium." Its point of departure is the theory that "somewhere in the umplumbed ocean depths there exists a highly developed kind of mollusk capable of emulating certain characteristics of those life forms it devours."[85] Jacobi embellished this notion with a paragraph-long reference to the panoply of evil, sea-dwelling deities led by Great Cthulhu. Yet when August Derleth—himself a master of the Lovecraftian pastiche—included the story in his 1962 Arkham House anthology, *Dark Mind, Dark Heart,* he deleted the Cthulhu passage and stripped the yarn of its Lovecraftian trappings. In 1972, this edited version was reprinted in *Disclosures in Scarlet,* Jacobi's third collection for Arkham House; four years later, the fan magazine *Fantasy Crossroads* #7 published the tale as originally written— untouched by Derleth's pen. A comparison of the two is instructive, for it shows how extensively Derleth altered the manuscript; he not only edited the story but also rewrote significant portions of it. Here, for instance, is Jacobi's original paragraph:

> "That was his original theory. In later years he apparently cloaked it with a pattern of demonology and what amounted to a modern adaptation of prehistoric superstition and folklore. He believed that these super undersea species are the incarnation of those Elder Gods who ruled the antediluvian deep and whose existence has been brought down to us in the dark myths and legends of a primitive past; that commanded by the great Cthulhu, they have lain dormant these eons in the sunken city of Flann, awaiting the time they would rise again to feed and rule. He believed further that this metempsychosis of the Elder Gods carried with it a latent incredible power and that if he could aid them to their destiny some of that power would be transmitted to him. Oh, Horatio really went all out in this mystic fol-de-rol. I even heard him promise his brother, Edmund, all kinds of maledictions if he continued to ridicule his beliefs."[86]

Under Derleth's editorial guidance, the following paragraphs replaced it:

> "That was his original theory. He embroidered it from time to time, and in his last years he grew pretty fanciful about it—got it all mixed up with demonology and folklore. Toward the end, Horatio went all out in this mystic fol-de-rol—talked about making sacrifices to his conch and all that rot—it was one of the things the brothers quarreled about. I overheard them more than once—Edmund ridiculing Horatio's beliefs, and Horatio calling down all kinds of maledictions on Edmund.
>
> "After Edmund had left, I asked Horatio on one occasion where his brother had gone. He just laughed and said Edmund went to prove—or disprove—his theories. 'He's gone far deeper into the subject than he ever thought he'd go—far deeper,' he said. And, of course, Edmund never did come back. I can't say I blame him. Who'd want to come back to live with a man clearly on the distaff side of sanity? Nothing was ever heard from Edmund after that."[87]

One should not infer from this that "The Aquarium"—a chilling horror story in either version—is any less effective in its more widely circulated format; it had borne but a passing reference to Cthulhu, and is quite capable of standing without it. What this does underscore is Derleth's propensity for taking liberties with many of the tales he published—Lovecraft's included.

During the Sixties and early Seventies, Arkham House brought out four additional Jacobi stories, three of them in anthologies edited by August Derleth. In "Kincaid's Car," which appeared in *Over the Edge* (1964), a railway boxcar containing "wish suppliers" from another world determines whether mankind is worthy of annexation by alien creatures. "The Unpleasantness at Carver House," featured in *Travellers By Night* (1967), ranks among Jacobi's finest exercises in pure, unrelenting horror: grotesque, life-sized statuary (clearly recalling the setting of "Revelations in Black"), generous doses of formaldehyde, and a shock ending make for strange goings-on in a moldy old mausoleum of a house in rural Carver County, Minnesota. Another tale calculated to set an icy worm crawling up the reader's spine is "The Cocomacaque," offered in the Winter, 1971, number of the Derleth-edited magazine, *The Arkham Collector*. In it, a bank robber pulls a heist at Victoria (another Carver County locale); it's a pushover, until he's stopped by a spectral figure wielding a Haitian war club—the village marshal, deceased for the past five years. In a wooded area near the Lake Bavaria road (still another Carver County setting), a Minneapolis film distributor discovers an odd wall surmounted by crude stone birds (also reminiscent of "Revelations in Black") and adorned with Romany designs to protect it from witchcraft; something white and formless darts into the woods—the mewling horror behind "The Singleton Barrier," which came out in *Dark Things* (1971).

A South American dictator is assassinated in "Exit Mr. Smith," published as "He Looked Back" in the August, 1966, issue of *If*; what makes his murder unusual is that it had been instigated by extraterrestrials. *The Saint Magazine* ran a detective yarn featuring Johnny Luang of the Malaysia Police, who investigates a royal murder and the disappearance of five sacred emeralds known as "The Keys of Kai" (May, 1967). Rounding out Jacobi's magazine appearances during this period was "The Player at Yellow Silence," an adroitly handled science-fantasy story set on a golf course, which agent Virginia Kidd sold to *Galaxy Magazine* (June, 1970). "He came out of nowhere like a summer storm and like thunder he went bowling down the fairways, breaking record after record."[88] But this unbeatable marvel is an emissary from an alien race, and at stake is the survival of humanity.

XIII

The years were slipping by. Jacobi had lived happily in his parents' home for more than fifty years. Suddenly he found himself alone. On 13 October 1965, his 89-year-old paternal aunt, Laura Emilie Jacobi, a former concert pianist who had lived nearby, died. Nine days later, on 22 October, his mother Matie had a heart attack and passed away at the age of 88. Carl quit his job at Honeywell on 20 October, and for two years a distraught Jacobi rattled about the old house in seclusion, his chief amusement that of chasing Higgins (a newly acquired kitten) off the mantlepiece or his father's piano. Gradually he cast his lethargy aside and finally turned to the novel he had always wanted to write.

"Mr. Jacobi is at work on a novel," Derleth proclaimed on the dust-jacket blurb for *Revelations in Black* in 1947. "Your comment ... that I am writing a novel brought a chuckle from me," Jacobi shot back. "What are you trying to do, force my hand? Now I suppose I'll have to do a booklength to keep up with this advertisement."[89] That's precisely what Derleth had in mind. Although Jacobi had outlined many novel-length plots during the Forties, he had always been forced to lay them aside and produce shorter stories to generate needed income. In 1944, he developed a plot for a juvenile adventure book set on the Gunflint Trail in Minnesota's north woods. Two years later, he wrote several chapters of a novel entitled *Captain Royal*, a well-researched costume romance of seventeenth-century France under Richelieu. Another 1946 plot was a whodunit set in Trinidad, with a detective named either Matthew or Jonathan Case. The year 1947 found him outlining *Mississippi Coach*, a regional historical novel of St. Anthony/Minneapolis and St. Paul in the 1850s. He applied for a University of Minnesota Regional Writing Fellowship in 1950, submitting an outline for an historical novel to be called *Gentleman of the Forest,* based on the life of explorer Daniel Greysolon, Sieur du Lhut. In 1952, he researched and plotted another book concerning sixteenth-century England and Cuba and the early exploration of Florida. The following year, he started a mystery novel entitled *Caribbean Assignment.* In 1956, he developed an outline for *River of the White Leopard*, a juvenile adventure with a Malaysian setting, and brushed up on his East Indies background; two years later, he began to dictate the story into a tape recorder, only to discover that he thinks visually rather than orally. Nothing ever came of any of these attempts. Project after project was postponed and then shelved; without steady magazine sales, he felt he couldn't afford to undertake a more sustained piece of work. But in December, 1967, he launched a juvenile mystery adventure laid in Carver County on Lake Minnewashta and the surrounding towns of Chaska and Excelsior, with one chapter set in Minneapolis—the same locales as those of "The Unpleasantness at Carver House," "The Cocomacaque", and "The Singleton Barrier." By the time he had completed the first 50,000-word draft in August, 1968, he had changed the title from *Romany Camp* to *The Jade Scorpion*. Most of the next fall was given to revision work and polishing, and by early winter, 1969, it was finished—longer by far than "Satan's Roadhouse" and "Cosmic Castaway," the lengthiest novelettes he'd ever written. Jacobi dedicated the book to August Derleth. It has not yet been published.

One of Carl Jacobi's most gratifying moments came when, in January, 1971, the University of Minnesota Libraries requested that he donate his plot outlines, synopses, original manuscripts, related correspondence, and extensive collection of pulp magazines to their Literary Manuscripts Collections. "We feel," their letter stated, "that this material would be of great value to researchers, both students and professional scholars, who are interested in studying the development of this genre of writing or your career in particular, as an outstanding Minnesota author."[90] Jacobi was delighted to honor their request, and his papers have been on permanent deposit there since 1972.[91]

August Derleth's death at the age of 62 from a heart attack, on 4 July 1971, was a great blow to Jacobi and many other writers.

> ...his letters had become a part of my life. Yet during the forty years or so we wrote to each other I saw him only a very few times when he was in Minneapolis, or rather St. Paul, visiting Don Wandrei. Though I regret it now I never did get down to Sauk City to visit him.
>
> But he remains in my memory as a loyal friend who went out of his way to give me encouragement and advice, who commented again and again and criticized my work when he had a thousand other things to do and who did much to bring my fantasy stories to light and to aid in their reprint and translation in many parts of the world.[92]

XIV

Misfortune had begun to stalk Carl Jacobi. In the autumn of 1971, he sustained a serious injury in a fall at home, and was rushed into an intensive-care unit suffering from shock. Two breathing arrests followed, and a tracheotomy was performed. Suspecting stroke, his doctors conducted a series of brain-wave tests; although one of the magazines later reported that he had suffered a stroke, Jacobi maintains that the tests proved negative. He had to learn to walk again, and remained hospitalized for nearly seven months.

In his absence, the house at 3717 4th Avenue South had been burgled. Jacobi returned home in the spring of 1972, to discover that thieves had backed a truck up to the front door and taken his typewriter, tape recorder, banjo, golf clubs, cameras, antique Christmas ornaments, all his boyhood toys, most of the furniture, and his father's coin collection and piano. His insurance company refused to cover the loss, ruling somewhat dubiously that the house had been vacant when the theft occurred. The neighborhood had been deteriorating for years, and Jacobi had considered moving for some time. Flooded with memories of the fifty-seven years he had spent there, he quickly sold the house and moved into an apartment on the opposite side of Minneapolis, at 507 Humboldt Avenue North.

Inactive for very nearly the first time in his career, Jacobi had emerged from the hospital a somber figure of a man—woven tightly into a cocoon of despondency, assailed by self-doubt, and hampered by the Parkinson's disease he had endured for thirty years. A nagging question gnawed at him: could he still write? He had tried to produce one story, "Cobb's Corridor," from his hospital bed, but it simply hadn't jelled. Initial efforts at the new apartment were just as discouraging. Stubbornly he persisted. Here he pays tribute to Carolyn Miles, the compassionate lady who restored his sagging self-confidence:

> She perhaps did more for me to make my return to writing possible after my long illness than any other person. We first met in her occupational therapy class. I had had surgery on my right hand, and to strengthen it the doctor had prescribed operation of a loom. After I left the hospital I was pretty much depressed. All attempts to plot a story now seemed beyond me, and every line of fiction I wrote seemed stilted and disconnected. Mrs. Miles struck first at the psychological core of this depression. Then night after night she drove from her home in St. Louis Park clear across town to my apartment in north

Minneapolis, and spent anywhere from two to three hours reading aloud my writings, analyzing my plots and making suggestions.

...I cannot express strongly enough my appreciation to Mrs. Miles, not only for lifting me out of the "slough of despond" but for returning me to the ranks of fictioneers. One simply can't appreciate what it means to a writer to have his brainchildren read aloud by someone with intellectual ability.[93]

It was a long pull, but he made it. Midway through "The Elcar Special," his first successfully completed short story since his illness, Jacobi asked old friend Clifford Simak to assess its merits. Relates Simak:

As well as charm and courtesy, the man has courage.... Carl was extremely ill, but after some months he fought back to better health. As soon as he was able physically to do it, he began writing again, although I know that he feared that the illness might have dimmed his skill. When he asked me to read the beginning of a story that he was writing, I shrunk from doing it, for there is no more pitiful thing than to find a man trying to continue a skill that has been lost. I need not have feared. The writing sang as it had of old; it still had the old Jacobi flair. He had, and still has, an individual hallmark that brands his work unmistakably as his own. One need not see the by-line to know that what he is reading is Jacobi.[94]

Shortly after many of his treasured pulps were stolen from the basement locker of his north Minneapolis apartment in 1973, Jacobi moved to another apartment at 3120 Hennepin Avenue South, his residence for the next nine years.

On the brighter side, Arkham House brought out his third collection of uncanny tales in 1972. He and August Derleth had originally mapped out the book's contents in 1966, and Jacobi had deliberately chosen the title *Disclosures in Scarlet* for its obvious similarity to *Revelations in Black* and *Portraits in Moonlight.* Substitutions made during the next several years led to the deletion of "Hamadryad Chair," "Double Trouble," "The Sangumenke" ("Death's Outpost"), and "The Lost Street" (the Simak-Jacobi collaboration originally entitled "The Street That Wasn't There"). Finally published the year after Derleth's death, the collection contained "The Aquarium," "The Player at Yellow Silence," "The Unpleasantness at Carver House," "The Cocomacaque," "The Gentleman Is an Epwa," "Strangers to Straba," "Exit Mr. Smith" ("He Looked Back"), "Gentlemen, the Scavengers," "The White

Pinnacle," "The War of the Weeds," "Kincaid's Car," "The Random Quantity," "The Singleton Barrier," and four previously unpublished tales: "The Royal Opera House," "Round Robin," "Mr. Iper of Hamilton," and "Sequence."

A parapsychologist uses telekinesis to prevent an environmental tragedy in "The Royal Opera House," begun in 1963 and rejected by *Amazing Stories* in 1966. Novels had been written in round-robin fashion before, but what makes this "Round Robin" unique is the fact that each of the collaborators comes from a different world; reminiscent of "Matthew South and Company," this classic science-fantasy tale of obsession, revenge, and suicide sports a decidedly unexpected ending and was originally penned as "The Satellite Writers" in 1966. "Mr. Iper of Hamilton," a Halloween yarn from the same period, offers a string of paper dolls dancing in the moonlight to the sweet music of a pied piper from another galaxy. "Sequence," a science-fiction story set on planet Nida 255 on the outer fringe of the unknown, had been turned down (under its original title, "The Visitors") in 1950 by Sam Merwin, Jr., at *Thrilling Wonder Stories.* Jacobi dedicated *Disclosures in Scarlet* to the memory of his mother.

Fritz Leiber's review in *Fantastic* said:

> His short stories show the sort of honest, unpretentious craftsmanship Derleth favored and fostered....
> His best tales in this book are horror rather than science fiction: "The Aquarium," "The Singleton Barrier" with all its grotesqueries, and that memorable tale of the dead-alive: "The Unpleasantness at Carver House."
> If there is one quality that distinguishes Jacobi's horror stories, it's that of the *grotesque,* which, incidentally, is a word derived from *grotto*—meaning the sort of shocking things you'd be apt to find in nooks, crypts, crannies, and humid and ferny and heavily shadowed rock gardens.[95]

In *The Magazine of Fantasy and Science Fiction,* Gahan Wilson called attention to the book's

> wide variety of Jacobian divertissements, my personal favorites being "The Aquarium," a really nasty piece of work, and a sentimental bit of necrophilia named, rather demurely, all things considered, "The Unpleasantness at Carver House."[96]

Literary agent Kirby McCauley echoed these sentiments in the

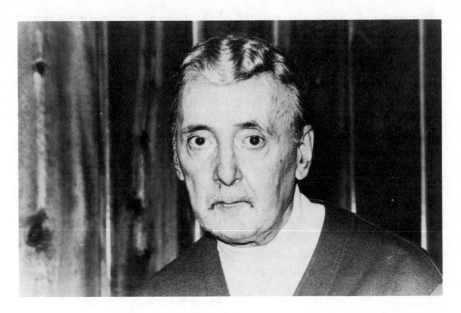

Carl (1972)
Photograph by Eric Carlson

Minneapolis Tribune, calling Jacobi "an authentic literary magician."[97]

One might quibble over the predominance given science fiction in this collection, or the presence of so many reprints from earlier Arkham House publications; but the inclusion of such spine-tinglers as "The War of the Weeds," "The Aquarium," "The Unpleasantness at Carver House," "The Singleton Barrier," and "Round Robin"— Jacobi at his finest and ghastliest—should be enough to satisfy any devotee of the bizarre.[98]

In 1973, Kirby McCauley persuaded Jacobi to attend the 32nd World Science Fiction Convention held over the Labor Day weekend (31 August-3 September) at the Royal York Hotel in Toronto. There, in Jacobi's hotel room, Carl and that master of the psychological horror story, Robert Bloch, met for the second time. Clifford Simak had introduced the two writers in 1943, when Bloch, who lived in Milwaukee, was in Minneapolis visiting Simak. Bloch recalls the Toronto encounter:

> The real revelation of our meeting lay in his graciousness and modesty. We talked, as might be expected, about the names that had meant magic in our youth—H. P. Lovecraft, Farnsworth Wright, August Derleth, Virgil Finlay—each of whom had played a part in our early professional careers. But it was only with difficulty that I persuaded Carl Jacobi to speak of his own work and of his present writing projects.[99]

XV

An event worth celebrating took place in the summer of 1973: the reappearance of that unique magazine of the macabre, *Weird Tales.* Jacobi had suggested in September, 1954, that August Derleth purchase all rights to the defunct pulp and issue it semiannually, if only to keep the magazine alive. Derleth showed no interest, but Leo Margulies did. The veteran publisher bought the rights to the magazine's title, bided his time cautiously, and finally put *Weird Tales* back on the newsstands in time to commemorate its 50th anniversary. Published in the standard 6½″ x 9¼″ pulp format, the magazine was edited by pulp fan and collector Sam Moskowitz, but distribution and sales were disappointing, and the revival succumbed after just four issues. Jacobi's "The Music Lover," which had been rejected by *Playboy* in 1968, came out in the final number (Summer, 1974); in it, a phonograph serves as the gateway to a surreal world of alter egos. Jacobi found out about the sale of this story under unusual circumstances. At the World Science Fiction Convention in Toronto, Clifford Simak introduced him to a room full of fans, authors, artists, publishers, and editors. "I'd like you to meet Carl Jacobi," Simak announced. "You all know his work." "I know," replied Sam Moskowitz. "I just bought a story from him."[100] This was the first Jacobi had heard of the acceptance.

He was back in stride. Arkham House published "Chameleon Town" in *Nameless Places,* a 1975 anthology edited by Gerald W. Page. It concerns a physician who encounters his wife and the man she had run off with—but they have both been dead for two years, and the town he saw them in hasn't existed since 1906. In "McIver's Fancy," which Kirby McCauley sold to *Mike Shayne Mystery Magazine* (December, 1976), an ancient Indian burial mound holds the key to a series of brutal slayings near Chaska in Carver County, Minnesota. Obeah worship and the psychic residue of a deadly hatred drive "The Elcar Special" to a shattering climax in Stuart Schiff's 1979 anthology, *Whispers II.* Publisher Stan Lee of the Marvel Comics Group had purchased the story for *The Haunt of Horror* in 1974, but the magazine soon began phasing out fiction and was unable to use it. (The real Elcar Special was a custom-built auto which daredevil exhibitionist Lillian Boyer used in her stunts during the Twenties. While he was still in high school, Jacobi saw her perform at the Minnesota State Fair: Boyer stood on the hood of the vehicle as it roared down the track at seventy miles an hour, grabbed a rope ladder dangling from a biplane which swooped down with a deafening roar, and made her ascent—a dangerous feat, for if the plane had lost altitude because of the sudden increase in weight, Boyer could easily have been dragged or run over.)

Jacobi also became active in the fan magazine field during the Seventies. Book dealer and pulp collector Robert Weinberg published "Eternity When?" in *WT50: A Tribute to Weird Tales* (1974); this short-short, about an old man who posts religious signs along the highway, dates from 1948 and was originally aimed at the slicks, but *Collier's, This Week, The American, The Blue Book Magazine* and *Best Years* had turned it down. "Hamadryad," a supernatural sea story set off the East Borneo coast, ran in the June, 1975, issue of Stuart Schiff's *Whispers;* it tells of a mysterious woman from Macassar and a closely guarded teakwood chest containing a priceless emerald—and a ten-foot king cobra. "Test Case," one of the most seductive science-fiction tales Jacobi has ever produced, came out in the Summer-Fall, 1975, number of Gary

Hoppenstand's *Midnight Sun.* Tension builds gradually and with insidious care as the town of Waconia in Carver County, Minnesota, is quietly sealed off from the rest of the world—no telephone, no radio or television, no bus or railroad, no incoming or outgoing cars; the community has been invaded by alien beings. *Fantasy Crossroads* # 7 published the unedited version of "The Aquarium" (February, 1976); *Starwind Magazine* reprinted "Canal" (Spring, 1976), calling it "a significant work in the development of modern science fiction"; and Robert Weinberg reprinted "Satan's Roadhouse" in *Weird Menace Classics*# 2 (1977). *Midnight Sun Five* brought out "Forsaken Voyage" (1979), one of Jacobi's personal favorites; another adventure yarn set at sea (this one off the coast of Honduras), it had lain in his files for years. Under its original title, "Forsaken Cruise," it was rejected by *Maclean's Magazine* of Toronto in 1941, and by Rogers Terrill at *Argosy* in 1943. A revised version entitled "Glory Passage" was accepted in 1950 by *Peace Force,* a magazine published on behalf of the United Nations, but which ceased publication before the story could be used; Cylvia Kleinman of *Short Stories Magazine* turned down another revised version, "The Last Cruise of the Trinidad Castle," in 1958, for the magazine was in the process of folding. Another yarn published many years after it was written is "The Syndicate of the Snake," a 1937 terror tale which came out in the second number of *Etchings and Odysseys* (1983).

Autobiographical pieces started to appear as well. "Memories of August" was featured in Tom Collins' *IS six* (1972); "Rambling Memoirs" came out in C.C. Clingan's *The Diversifier* (July, 1977), "The Derleth Connection" in *The August Derleth Society Newsletter* (June, 1981), and "Some Correspondence" in *Etchings and Odysseys'* second issue (1983). Jacobi also contributed a foreword to a 1977 chapbook, *Carl Jacobi: An Appreciation,* edited by William H. Pugmire; in it, J. Vernon Shea, Hugh B. Cave, Mary Elizabeth Counselman, Clifford D. Simak, E. Hoffmann Price, Fritz Leiber, and Robert Bloch paid tribute to a master.

XVI

In such tales as "The Nameless City" (1921), "The Festival" (1923), and "The Call of Cthulhu" (1926), H. P. Lovecraft began to refer to certain fictitious books—crumbling volumes wholly unintelligible to all but the most knowledgeable students of witchcraft, sorcery, and the occult—to which he imparted the semblance of credibility by providing detailed bibliographic data. Of these books (which, purportedly, few had seen, but of which much was whispered), none was as abhorrent as the dreaded *Necronomicon* of the mad Arab, Abdul Alhazred. *Al Azif* (the original Arabic title), written in Damascus circa A. D. 730, was translated into Greek as the *Necronomicon* in 950 by Theodorus Philetas; in 1050, nearly all copies of the Greek edition were burnt by Patriarch Michael; Olaus Wormius translated the Greek text into Latin in 1228, but both versions were suppressed by Pope Gregory IX in 1232. Lovecraft expanded the bibliography in such short stories and novelettes as "The Case of Charles Dexter Ward" (1927), "The Colour out of Space" (1927), "The Dunwich Horror" (1929), "The Whisperer in Darkness" (1930), "At the Mountains of Madness" (1931), "The Shadow over Innsmouth" (1931), "The Dreams in the Witch-House" (1932), "The Thing on the Doorstep" (1933), "The Shadow out of Time" (1934), and "The Haunter of the Dark" (1935). Monstrously supplementing the *Necronomicon* were such unspeakable works as the *Pnakotic Manuscripts,* the *R'lyeh Text,* and the *Book of Dzyan.* Members of the Lovecraft circle added forbidden titles of their own, and delighted in borrowing each other's inventions (as did HPL himself): Clark Ashton Smith contributed the accursed *Book of Eibon* (or *Liber Ivoris),* Robert E. Howard the hideous *Unaussprechlichen Kulten* of Fvindvuf von Junzt (the mad German poet and philosopher); Robert Bloch gave us Ludvig Prinn's frightful *De Vermis Mysteriis,* August Derleth the fiendish *Celaeno Fragments* and the unmentionable *Cultes des Goules* of the Comte d'Erlette. Long after Lovecraft's death, J. Ramsey Campbell introduced *The Revelations of Glaaki,* while fellow Britisher Brian Lumley concocted the hellish *Cthaat Aquadingen* and the sinister *G'harne Fragments.*

To this imaginative library of fearsome lore, Carl Jacobi added his own shelf of ghoulish delights, including *Twenty Experiments in the Occult*; the banned *Gypsy Zenicaron;* Bentley's *Beyond the Mundane;* Herzog's *Furchtbare Kulte;* Le Loyer's *Book of Spectres;*[101] Milo Calument's *I Am a Werewolf,* "all copies of which...were supposed to have been cast in Hoxton marsh";[102] *The Dark Elements of Survival,* "dealing with eighteenth-century sorcery in some of its ugliest forms,"[103] specifically "the postponement of death by occult means";[104] Gantley's *Hydrophinnae,* "containing some of the most hideous and horrible illustrations...ever seen";[105] *Dwellers in the Depths* by Gaston Le Fe, "who, the foreword stated quite blandly, had died insane";[106] a

pirated German manuscript, *Unter Zee Kulten,* "all copies of which
had supposedly been destroyed in the seventeenth century";[107] and
Elixir of Life by Giuseppe Balsamo, the mysterious Count
Cagliostro (1743-1795). But the most outre is Richard Verstegan's
Restitution of Decayed Intelligence, "long ago banned by God-
fearing people as being inspired by Satan."[108] Jacobi introduced it
in "The Face in the Wind," written in 1933, and "quoted" from it at
length:

> And Neptune and Terra had three daughters. And their
> names were Celaeno, Aello, and Ocypete. But theye were
> offspring accursed, for theye were winged monsters with the
> face of a woman and the bodys of vultures. Theye emitted an
> infectious smell and spoiled whatever theye touched bye their
> filth. Theye were harpies![109]

The book also figures in "The Phantom Pistol," "The Corbie Door,"
"The Random Quantity," "The Unpleasantness at Carver House,"
"The Singleton Barrier," and "The Black Garden." Curiously
enough, although the passage "quoted" in "The Face in the Wind" is
pure fabrication, its "source," *Restitution of Decayed Intelligence,*
actually exists.[110] Here Jacobi discusses its role in his career:

> I suppose most fantasy writers have at one time or another
> created the title of a book to promote some theory of witchcraft or
> supernatural postulation. I can lay claim to a few, including *I
> Am a Werewolf, Hydrophinnae, Dwellers in the Depths,* and
> *Unter Zee Kulten.* These of course are all fictitious books, yet *I
> Am a Werewolf* brought me at least five requests that I inform
> them where this book could be obtained.[111] I also had the
> satisfaction of having the three other books used by the British
> writer, Brian Lumley, in one of his stories.
> But my favorite is *Restitution of Decayed Intelligence* by
> Richard Verstegan. I don't know when I first stumbled upon
> mention of this book. It was sometime in the early Thirties. My
> source said the book had been banned and most copies destroyed
> in the eighteenth century. I believe I first used it in "The Face in
> the Wind." Since very few persons have ever heard of the book, I
> always thought of it as my own discovery. It was listed under the
> authorship of Verstegan, but with a secondary name of
> Rowlands. Reference books also list it as Richard Rowlands'
> version of his friend Verstegan's writing. On the binding of the
> copy I obtained is the name Rowlands, but there are several
> short forewords by Verstegan (reproduced with his signature).
> Not only is the writing difficult to read because of the Old
> English typography, but the text is so garbled I found it difficult
> indeed.[112]

XVII

In 1976, thieves ransacked Jacobi's lake cabin at Red Cedar Point and made off with many valuable books, pulps, and phonograph records, a Rochester lamp, a phonograph, and a settee that Carl had refinished himself. He hadn't spent much time there for some years and the untended grounds had begun to look like the jungles of Bataan. In 1962, he had sold his Chevrolet, which he had driven home—glittering and spanking new—from the display rooms in 1935. Transportation had been an ordeal ever since. To reach the cabin, he had to take three buses, one of which wound halfway around Lake Minnetonka, then call for a country taxi from the nearest town, Excelsior, for the three-mile ride to Lake Minnewashta; for the return trip, he would have to make arrangements for the cab to pick him up, and time the whole operation to catch the last bus back to Minneapolis. He had considered selling the place for nearly twenty years, and finally did in 1977, after the costs of road paving and installation of sewers, telephone and electric lines made it impossible to keep up. The cabin has since been razed.

Besides Hugh B. Cave (who moved to Sebastian, Florida, after selling his Jamaican coffee plantation in 1974, and whose collection, *Murgunstrumm and Others,* was published by Carcosa in 1977), Jacobi's most frequent correspondents today are two other distinguished veterans of the pulp era: Mary Elizabeth Counselman (1911-   ) of Gadsden, Alabama, and E. Hoffmann Price (1898-   ) of Redwood City, California. Thirty of Counselman's stories appeared in *Weird Tales* between 1933 and 1953—including the acclaimed supernatural classic, "The Three Marked Pennies" (August, 1934), recently reprinted in her 1978 Arkham House collection, *Half in Shadow.* She recalls meeting Jacobi at the Radisson Hotel in Minneapolis in 1973:

> I met Carl Jacobi rather late in our *Weird Tales* and Arkham House affiliations, in comparison with earlier contacts by mail with Seabury Quinn, Greye La Spina, Harold Lawlor and, of course, our friend and mentor, August Derleth.
>
> We empathized at once because both of us were greatly attached to overpowering fathers, and because we both had worked on a newspaper. On a visit to Minneapolis in 1973, to recover my equilibrium after my mother's sudden death in surgery, I called Carl the minute I landed. He sounded shy over the phone. Kirby McCauley brought him to my hotel, and we

Carolyn Miles (1980)

E. Hoffmann Price and Carl (1973)
Photograph by Eric Carlson

took to each other immediately. We spent the evening comparing magazine appearances, gossiping about our fellow fantasy greats, and swapping "Do-you-remember?" reminiscences.[113]

The prolific Price—author of the collections, *Strange Gateways* (Arkham House, 1967) and *Far Lands Other Days* (Carcosa, 1975)— was also in the Twin Cities in 1973, visiting Don Wandrei in St. Paul. Jacobi and Price got together at Kirby McCauley's apartment in Minneapolis, where they exchanged nostalgic recollections and formed a lasting friendship.

XVIII

Carl Jacobi has been writing for a half century and more, and is still an active fictioneer. Two of his latest eerie yarns helped kick off the *Weird Tales* paperback series for Zebra Books (Robert Weinberg had purchased the rights to the magazine's title after the Margulies-Moskowitz experiment failed in 1974). "If I were you, I'd just leave it alone."[114] Dead Man's Pit, that is—the one where that boy, one of the finest swimmers in Carver County, had drowned the year before. Originally titled "The Chadwick Pit," but shortened to "The Pit" by editor Lin Carter for its appearance in *Weird Tales* # 1 (1980), this story of a centuries-old death cult dates from the mid-Seventies; shorn of its supernatural trappings, it sold as a straight mystery ("McIver's Fancy") to *Mike Shayne Mystery Magazine*. "The Black Garden" (*Weird Tales* #3, 1981) is located in Cologne, which had been a peaceful farming community in Carver County until it was discovered that the mysterious woman in black has been raising plants that feed on the blood of young virgins—the final wedge of horror in an already terrifying tale.

Awaiting a publisher is Jacobi's new fantasy collection, *Smoke of the Snake*. It promises plenty of nightmares, for, besides the title story, it contains "The Music Lover," "Hamadryad," "The Elcar Special," "Eternity When?," "The Keys of Kai," "The Lost Street" ("The Street That Wasn't There"), "The Black Garden," "Test Case," "The Jade Scarlotti," "Chameleon Town," "The Chadwick Pit" ("The Pit"), and three unpublished tales from the Seventies: "The Tunnel" (bought for 6¢ a word by *Midnight Sun* in 1975, but unused at the time the magazine folded), "Offspring," and "A Quire of Foolscap." In addition to a handful of stories he has turned out during the past several years ("A Letter to Sarah," "The Lavalier," and "The Riburi Hat"), he would also like to guide into print *East of*

Samarinda, a collection of his briskly paced East Indies adventure yarns, featuring such top-flight tales as "Holt Sails the 'San Hing'," "Crocodile," "Black Passage," "Deceit Post," "Jungle Wires," "Leopard Tracks," "Tiger Island," "Quarry," "Sumpitan," "A Film in the Bush," "Submarine I-26," "Letter of Dismissal," "Spider Wires," "Redemption Trail," "Hamadryad Chair," and the title yarn—each one every bit as suspenseful as Jacobi's work in the macabre. Writes E. Hoffmann Price:

> ...I am looking forward to Carl's breaking into the paperback novel field. From old times, I have been impressed by his authentic and colorful adventure stories of Indonesia-Borneo. Having soldiered in Luzon in 1917 and having researched much of Carl's territory (story locales), I found his narratives most appealing. I have taken the liberty of suggesting to him that with his background experience, he could readily switch from shorts and novelettes to booklengths, through skilful presentation of subplots, or putting on scene matters he used to keep offstage in short narratives.[115]

But this is another story, one that will be held over until its proper time for telling.

XIX

He cut his teeth on the pulps, which thrilled and chilled the masses and catered to the tastes of readers eager for inexpensive, light fiction of a sensational nature—escapist entertainment, paced with relentless ferocity and serving up solid, hard-core mayhem. Amid the snappy synonyms guaranteeing the weirdest and eeriest, the most thrilling and startling, one might hardly expect to find literature of enduring merit.

Yet Carl Jacobi is an acknowledged master of the macabre. Among devotees of the supernatural, the weird, and the fantastic, he holds an honored place as one of America's foremost authors of imaginative fiction. Why? What makes a Jacobi yarn special? Jacobi tells us:

> To me there is one unbreakable rule in successful fiction writing. If your chief character's actions are fantastic or removed from reality, then your background should be commonplace. If your backdrop is a strange world, a far distant planet, or an antediluvian period of the Earth's past, then your protagonist should be an ordinary fellow with ordinary traits

R. Dixon Smith and Carl (10 October 1982)
Photograph by Eric Carlson

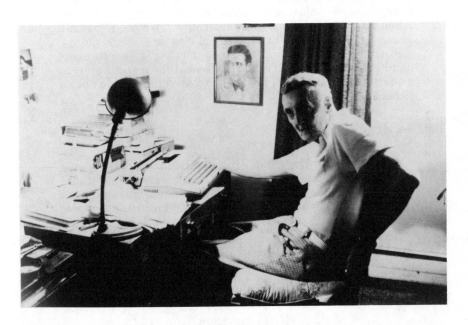

Carl (10 October 1982)
Photograph by Eric Carlson

and characteristics. If you have both in the same story (as some sword and sorcery tales do), it is difficult for your reader to have something which he can relate to.[116]

These principles Jacobi applies to the traditional tale of terror. Those set in rural Carver County, for instance, contain placid, conventional, recognizable locales, offsetting the disturbing occurrences with which these communities are confronted.

Jacobi holds the distinction of being one of the most polished practitioners in his field. His tales bear the imprint of a disciplined approach to the writing of fiction. His insistence on thorough background research and accurate detail bespeaks a careful craftsmanship rarely found in this type of story. As a result of his time-consuming devotion to revision, his output has never been high, but his average of sales balanced against written copy is most impressive. He once told Mary Elizabeth Counselman:

> ...I won't let a story go out of these diggings until I've revised it, edited it, and made it as good a product as I possibly can. The result is that I've been far from prolific in the past, but I've sold just about everything I've ever written. True, sometimes they haven't sold for years, but eventually they did find a market. That is, excepting the out-and-out duds which I knew were lousy and which in most cases I didn't even try to sell. I was talking to a chap here one time who was appalled when I told him how long it had taken me to write one particular story. "Why hell," he said, "I can bang out a story in a quarter of that time." "And did you sell it?" I asked. "Noooo," he said, "but that's because some dumb editor just didn't like it." Well, I could "bang out" a story in a quarter of that time too, and probably an editor wouldn't like it either.[117]

Relates Hugh B. Cave:

> Very early in the game I came to realize Carl was doing something few other writers of fantasy were doing, and I admired it and tried to learn from it. He was saying more in ten words than most writers of the time were saying in fifty, and was doing so by taking the time to find the one word that would hit home.
>
> This was unusual. Pulp writers as a rule—those of us, anyway, who were struggling to make a living at it—seldom took the time to do more than rough-polish a rough draft. Carl really polished, and is still doing so.[118]

The hallmark of a Jacobi story, then, is its succinctness and economy, a style derived in part from the work of Somerset Maugham—the only writer he has ever wished to emulate. A Jacobi narrative is spare and restrained, its style simple and direct, its power gentle and subtle, imbued with a vivid sense of the dramatic and an altogether unnerving mastery of narrative structure and thematic development. From the onset of the attention-grabbing opening paragraph, the pace begins rather slowly, increasing gradually as the tale progresses and the atmosphere darkens; until suddenly the full impact of what has been but half suggested, vaguely hinted at, or merely suspected, screeches to a climax in the form of a shocking revelation. A perfect example of this steady, quiet unfolding of suspense ("just enough revealed, just enough concealed," as Robert E. Howard put it)[119] is found in that classic narrative of necrophilia, "The Unpleasantness at Carver House." Hugh B. Cave has remarked, "The buildup is beautiful, and all the clues are in place to warn the reader what's coming, yet the ending has the wallop of a sledgehammer all the same."[120] Jacobi's style, notes Mary Elizabeth Counselman, is matter-of-fact, almost reportorial, convincing the reader that what he or she has just read "*could* or *did* really happen."[121] This technique of understatement is equally evident in "Test Case," the science-fiction yarn in which extraterrestrials, disguised as workmen, visit the town of Waconia, Minnesota. Only once is any irregularity in their appearance mentioned, when a sheriff notices that one of the workmen has strangely elongated ears. And then Jacobi undercuts it with sly, ironic wit. " 'Looks like a damned wolf,' the sheriff muttered. 'This country should enforce its immigration laws. There's too many foreigners here.' "[122] Simple, subtle, and effective.

Jacobi's first two Arkham House collections are long out of print and are avidly sought by collectors. His stories are anthologized again and again, both here and abroad, in paperback and hard cover alike. The 1974 Neville Spearman hardbound reprint of *Revelations in Black* in England, followed by a two-volume British paperback edition in 1977 and an American paperback in 1979, introduced new generations of readers, too young to have read the pulps, to stories long unavailable. Fads and trends, however, mystify Jacobi. He wonders why the works of pulp writers Edgar Rice Burroughs and Louis L'Amour are perennially popular, while those of Alexandre Dumas and Rafael Sabatini are less so. Several of Jacobi's adventure yarns—"Crocodile" and "The Jade Scarlotti" come immediately to mind—are at least as entertaining as, if not superior to, many of his fantasy tales. Yet not one of them has ever been reprinted. Although fully a third of Jacobi's published output is adventure, none of it has been mined. There's still gold in the Rentharpian hills. Whether fantasy or adventure, we clamor for more.

Today, in his new uptown apartment at 3305 Hennepin Avenue South (to which he moved in the fall of 1982), Carl Jacobi continues to work. He confesses that he thoroughly enjoys a good cigar, but, happily, his first love remains his writing. Fortunately for the rest of us, he's still pounding a typewriter, and he's still writing stories as chilling as ever.

Notes

[1] Letter, Jacobi to Mary Elizabeth Counselman, 24 July 1981.

[2] *Ibid.*

[3] They moved to 3420 1st Avenue South in 1909, lived at 2721 Stevens Avenue from 1910 to 1913, and moved again, to 3010 2nd Avenue South, in 1914.

[4] Letter, Jacobi to author, 18 March 1982.

[5] *Ibid.*

[6] Jacobi, "The Derelict," in *The Quest* (Vol. 3, No. 2, May, 1925), p. 41.

[7] Letter, Jacobi to author, 18 March 1982. All three covers had been illustrated by Andrew Brosnatch: "Monsters of the Pit" (June, 1925), "The Werewolf of Ponkert" (July, 1925), and "The Stolen Body" (November, 1925).

[8] *Ibid.*

[9] *Ibid.*

[10] Undated letter, Jacobi to Counselman, March, 1982.

[11] Letter, Jacobi to author, 18 March 1982.

[12] Jacobi, "Mive," in *Weird Tales* (Vol. XIX, No. 1, January, 1932), p. 113.

[13] Letter, Derleth to Jacobi, 30 December 1931.

[14] H. P. Lovecraft, *Selected Letters: 1932-1934*, ed. August Derleth and James Turner (Sauk City, Wisconsin: Arkham House Publishers, Inc., 1976), pp. 24-25.

[15] Jacobi, "The Derleth Connection," in *The August Derleth Society Newsletter*, ed. Richard H. Fawcett (Vol. 4, No. 4, June, 1981), p. 4.

[16] Jacobi, "Memories of August," in *IS six,* ed. Tom Collins (1972), p. 26.

[17] Letter, Derleth to Jacobi, 7 December 1931.

[18] Jacobi, "Memories of August," p. 27.

[19] Jacobi, "The Derleth Connection," p. 6.

[20] Letter, Jacobi to author, 18 March 1982.

[21] Robert Kenneth Jones, *The Shudder Pulps: A History of the Weird Menace Magazines of the 1930's* (West Linn, Oregon: FAX Collector's Editions, Inc., 1975), p. xiv.

[22] Hugh B. Cave, *Murgunstrumm and Others* (Chapel Hill, North Carolina: Carcosa, 1977), p. x.

[23] Jacobi was paid twice for this story. Editor Harry Bates had bought it for *Strange Tales* in 1932, and had paid Jacobi $240.00 for its use, but the magazine was discontinued before the tale could be published. Jacobi then sold the story to Farnsworth Wright at *Weird Tales* for $120.00, after Wright had initially rejected it.

[24] This one sold the third time around. Farnsworth Wright found it unconvincing the first two times he read it, and returned the manuscript to Jacobi for revision. The changes were not made, as Wright's 6 June 1934 letter of acceptance makes clear.

[25] Jacobi, "Memories of August," p. 26.

[26] Jacobi, "The Derleth Connection," p. 4.

[27] W. H. Pugmire, ed., *Carl Jacobi: An Appreciation* (Pensacola, Florida: Stellar Z Productions, 1977), p. 7.

[28] Jacobi, "The Derleth Connection," p. 5.

[29] Letter, Jacobi to author, 18 March 1982.

³⁰Place-names are given here as Jacobi spelled them, according to the usage at the time, although the spellings of some have changed since then.

³¹Jacobi, "Memories of August," p. 28. Jacobi posted his letter on 6 February 1934, and received the reply, dated 15 September 1934, on 10 November of that year.

³²Letter, Jacobi to Derleth, 24 June 1937. Jacobi mailed his letter on 5 January 1937; the reply was dated 29 March of that year.

³³Letter, Jacobi to Derleth, 19 January 1940.

³⁴Jacobi, "The Derleth Connection," p. 5.

³⁵Letter, Jacobi to Derleth, 21 January 1948.

³⁶While gathering background information for this story in 1933, Jacobi discovered that, although Tiger Island actually exists (under the names Wuvulu or Maty), its existence was not known to the U.S. Navy, the British Admiralty Hydrographic Department, or the Ordnance Survey at Southampton, England. There the matter stood for more than forty years, until Jacobi heard motion-picture actor William Holden reveal in a late-Seventies interview that he owned property on Wuvulu.

³⁷The relay station (No. 5) which figures in "Jungle Wires" and "Spider Wires" was Jacobi's own invention. There was no Dutch East Borneo Telegraph Company.

³⁸Another story that sold twice. Farnsworth Wright had purchased a longer version for *Oriental Stories,* only to return the manuscript when the magazine (retitled *The Magic Carpet Magazine*) was temporarily discontinued, promising to buy it back at a later date. Jacobi, however, cut 2,500 words out of the yarn and sold it to *Complete Stories,* which had originally rejected it.

³⁹Letter, Jacobi to author, 18 March 1982.

⁴⁰Jacobi, "Rambling Memoirs," in *The Diversifier,* ed. C. C. Clingan (Vol. III, No. 5, July, 1977), p. 32.

⁴¹Jacobi, "The Derleth Connection," pp. 5-6.

⁴²Letter, Jacobi to Derleth, 18 November 1940.

⁴³Letter, Jacobi to Derleth, 29 September 1941.

⁴⁴Letter, Jacobi to Derleth, 26 July 1939.

⁴⁵Letters, Jacobi to author, 15 and 22 May 1982.

⁴⁶Another story for which Jacobi was paid twice. Harry Bates had purchased a longer version for *Strange Tales* in 1932, and had paid Jacobi $160.00 for its use, but the magazine folded before the yarn could be published. Jacobi cut 3,000 words from the manuscript in 1939, his agent Lurton Blassingame sold the story to *Weird Tales* in November of that year, and Jacobi received $45.00 for it in January, 1941.

⁴⁷Letter, Jacobi to author, 18 March 1982.

⁴⁸Letter, Jacobi to Derleth, 10 May 1941.

⁴⁹Letter, Jacobi to Derleth, 29 September 1941.

⁵⁰Letters, Jacobi to author, 15 and 22 May 1982.

⁵¹After the war, membership picked up a bit, but organizationally, little really survived except long-standing friendships.

⁵²Letter, Jacobi to author, 22 May 1982.

⁵³Letter, Jacobi to Derleth, 21 October 1942.

⁵⁴Letter, Jacobi to Derleth, 23 October 1944.

⁵⁵Letter, Jacobi to Derleth, 30 August 1945.

⁵⁶Letter, Jacobi to Derleth, 30 July 1945.

⁵⁷Jacobi in a letter to Derleth dated 30 August 1943: "...I suppose if Malcolm Reiss takes it, he'll change the title to 'Skylords of the Hyper-Sphere' or something like that."

⁵⁸In a letter dated 7 March 1946, Jacobi informed Derleth: "Malcolm Reiss of *Planet Stories* sent back 'The Nebula and the Necklace,' with a long and vague letter asking for revision. He said if I could change it according to his ideas, he'd take it; trouble is, he didn't know what those ideas were, save that the plot was a little too 'pat.' Of course it's pat; that's the type of plot his magazine uses." Then, on 18 April 1946: "That idiot, Malcolm Reiss, sent back 'The Nebula and the Necklace,' after I had completely rewritten it in accordance with his suggestions. This is the first and the only time a manuscript has failed to sell after requested revision. His reason? That he couldn't reorganize his mind into writing an acceptance after once giving the story a negative. I sent it to Margulies, but since it was an obvious sequel I haven't much hope."

⁵⁹Jacobi, "Tepondicon," in *Planet Stories* (Vol. III, No. 5, Winter Issue, September-November, 1946), p. 47.

⁶⁰Jacobi on Leo Margulies and John W. Campbell, Jr., in a letter to Derleth dated 21 September 1942: "One would think that with the many writers going into the service, editors

would let down the bars a trifle, or at least be less aloof. Not so. Leo turned down two perfectly good western shorts for little or no reason, save that my name isn't known in that field. Meanwhile, I understand that John Campbell at *Astounding* has been buying right and left from his regular writers before they left for the army, with the result that he now has a full inventory for that magazine. Campbell, incidentally, is a queer egg. He's made a rather nice magazine out of *Astounding* and certainly has improved *Unknown,* though I don't care particularly for it. But he simply won't buy from an agent. He likes to seize upon an utterly new writer and build him up in his own fashion."

[61]Jacobi acknowledged Derleth's assistance in a letter to him dated 9 December 1944: "I am in wholehearted accord with the new copy and regard it in all details a great improvement. And I have just enough self-ego for my own writing and regard for your analytical ability to say that I don't think there is another writer of weirds in the entire field but Derleth who could prompt such a remark from me. I hope McIlwraith likes it."

[62]Letter, Jacobi to Derleth, 14 February 1943.

[63]Letter, Jacobi to Derleth, 17 April 1953.

[64]Jacobi, "Rambling Memoirs," p. 32.

[65]Letter, Jacobi to Derleth, 6 August 1945.

[66]Letter, Jacobi to Derleth, 30 August 1945.

[67]Bloch, "Through a Glass, Darkly," in *The Arkham Sampler,* ed. August Derleth (Vol. 1, No. 1, Winter, 1948), pp. 84-86.

[68]Jacobi, "The Historian," in *Startling Stories* (Vol. 21, No. 2, May, 1950), p. 139.

[69]Letter, Jacobi to Derleth, 26 December 1949.

[70]Letter, Jacobi to Derleth, 16 January 1950. (The Campbell referred to is, of course, John W. Campbell, Jr.)

[71]Letter, Jacobi to Derleth, 4 May 1954.

[72]Letter, Jacobi to Derleth, 6 April 1950.

[73]Letter, Jacobi to Derleth, 26 March 1956.

[74]Letter, Jacobi to Derleth, 20 November 1960.

[75]Letter, Jacobi to Derleth, 24 June 1961.

[76]Letter, Jacobi to Derleth, 24 March 1962.

[77]Jacobi, "Strangers to Straba," in *Fantastic Universe* (Vol. 2, No. 3, October, 1954), p. 98.

[78]Jacobi, "Introducing the Author," in *Imagination* (Vol. 5, No. 8, August, 1954), p. 77.

[79]Pugmire, *op. cit.,* p. 4.

[80]*Ibid.,* pp. 3-4.

[81]Letter, Jacobi to Derleth, 11 March 1955.

[82]Letter, Jacobi to Derleth, 23 April 1955.

[83]Letter, Jacobi to Derleth, 1 June 1962.

[84]Letter, Jacobi to Derleth, 28 July 1962.

[85]Jacobi, "The Aquarium," in August Derleth, ed., *Dark Mind, Dark Heart* (Sauk City, Wisconsin: Arkham House Publishers, 1962), p. 143.

[86]Jacobi, "The Aquarium," in *Fantasy Crossroads* #7, ed. Jonathan Bacon (February, 1976), p. 21.

[87]Jacobi, "The Aquarium," in *Dark Mind, Dark Heart,* p. 143.

[88]Jacobi, "The Player at Yellow Silence," in *Galaxy Magazine* (Vol. 30, No. 3, June, 1970), p. 5.

[89]Letter, Jacobi to Derleth, 27 October 1947.

[90]Letter, Alan K. Lathrop to Jacobi, 22 January 1971.

[91]In the Literary Manuscripts Collections of the Manuscripts Division of the University of Minnesota Libraries. The papers of Clifford D. Simak and Gordon R. Dickson are also housed there.

[92]Jacobi, "Memories of August," p. 29.

[93]Letter, Jacobi to author, 28 May 1982.

[94]Pugmire, *op. cit.,* p. 12.

[95]*Fantastic* (Vol. 25, No. 4, August, 1976), p. 115.

[96]*The Magazine of Fantasy and Science Fiction* (Vol. 45, No. 6, December, 1973), p. 41.

[97]*Minneapolis Tribune,* March 25, 1973, p. 10D.

[98]In an unusual oversight, the book's copyright information appeared on the wrong page, and the U.S. Copyright Office refused to accept the book for copyright because of the misprint. As a result, *Disclosures in Scarlet*—and especially its four never-before-published stories—has never been protected by copyright and has always been in the public domain. Fortunately, however, Jacobi was paid for the use of "The Royal Opera House" when it was reprinted in the 1978 paperback, *Rod Serling's Other Worlds.*

[99]Bloch, "The Black Revealer," in *Midnight Sun Five,* ed. Gary Hoppenstand (1979), p. 28.

[100]Conversation, Jacobi with author, 7 November 1982.

[101]This one actually does exist. Pierre Le Loyer (1550-1634) wrote *Livre des Spectres* in 1586; a variant version entitled *discours et histoires des Spectres* appeared in 1605, followed by *discours des Spectres* in 1608; an English translation, *A Treatise of Spectres,* was published in London in 1605.

[102]Jacobi, "The Phantom Pistol," in *Weird Tales* (Vol. 35, No. 9, May, 1941), p. 67.

[103]Jacobi, "The Unpleasantness at Carver House," in August Derleth, ed., *Travellers By Night* (Sauk City, Wisconsin: Arkham House Publishers, 1967), p. 129.

[104]Jacobi, "The Black Garden," in Lin Carter, ed., *Weird Tales #3* (New York: Zebra Books/Kensington Publishing Corp., 1981), p. 150.

[105]Jacobi, "The Aquarium," in *Dark Mind, Dark Heart,* p. 141.

[106]*Ibid.*

[107]*Ibid.*

[108]Jacobi, "The Face in the Wind," in *Weird Tales* (Vol. 27, No. 4, April, 1936), p. 415.

[109]*Ibid.,* p. 416.

[110]Richard Verstegen (Jacobi spelled it "Verstegan") was the pseudonym of Richard Rowlands. *A Restitution of Decayed Intelligence: In antiquities. Concerning the most noble and renowned English nation.* By the Studie and trauaile of R. V., was printed in Antwerp and published in London in 1605.

[111]"Moreover, there were frequent applications to booksellers and libraries for the books of the Mythos, particularly the mythical *Necronomicon,* which some readers refused to believe was wholly imaginary. Dealers had a field day of their own, perpetrating the hoax, by advertising either for the *Necronomicon* or offering it for sale in sober advertisements like Walker Baylor's in the *Antiquarian Bookman*—'Alhazred, Abdul. *The Necronomicon.* Spain, 1647. Calf covers rubbed and some foxing, otherwise very nice condition. Many small woodcuts of mystic signs and symbols. Seems to be a treatise (in Latin) on Ritualistic Magic. Ex. lib. stamp on front fly leaf states that the book has been withdrawn from the Miskatonic University Library. Best offer.' " August Derleth, ed., "H. P. Lovecraft and His Work," in *The Dunwich Horror and Others: The Best Supernatural Stories of H. P. Lovecraft* (Sauk City, Wisconsin: Arkham House Publishers, 1963), p. xviii.

[112]Letter, Jacobi to author, 23 May 1982.

[113]Letter, Counselman to author, 14 May 1982.

[114]Jacobi, "The Pit," in Lin Carter, ed., *Weird Tales# 1* (New York: Zebra Books/Kensington Publishing Corp., 1980), p. 132.

[115]Letter, Price to author, 13 January 1983.

[116]Jacobi, "The Derleth Connection," p. 6.

[117]Letter, Jacobi to Counselman, 17 November 1975.

[118]Pugmire, *op. cit.,* p. 7.

[119]Letter praising "Mive," published in correspondence column "The Eyrie," in *Weird Tales* (Vol. XIX, No. 3, March, 1932), p. 414.

[120]Pugmire, *op. cit.,* pp. 7-8.

[121]Letter, Counselman to author, 14 May 1982.

[122]Jacobi, "Test Case," in *Midnight Sun,* ed. Gary Hoppenstand (Vol. 1, No. 2, Summer-Fall, 1975), p. 93.

Appendix I
Carl Jacobi
A Bibliography

Appendix I

Carl Jacobi: A Bibliography

All first appearances are listed, as well as most reprints and many foreign translations. However, there are undoubtedly some reprints, and especially foreign translations, which have escaped the author's attention. Corrections and additions are welcomed, and may be addressed to the author in care of the publisher.

Items are arranged chronologically—published works by date of publication, unpublished works by date of composition.

I. *High School and College Publications*

A. *Central High School*

"The Runaway Box-Car," *The Quest* (Vol. 3, No. 1, December, 1924), pp. 16-18. Adventure. 1,300 words.

"The Derelict," *The Quest* (Vol. 3, No. 2, May, 1925), pp. 40-41. Atmospheric vignette. 850 words.

"The Lost Tapestry," *The Quest* (Vol. 4, No. 1, December, 1925), pp. 11-13. Adventure. 1,250 words.

"The War of the Sun Dials," *The Quest* (Vol. 4, No. 2, June, 1926), pp. 9-12. Fantasy. 1,900 words.

"Ultra," *The Quest* (Vol. 5, No. 1, December, 1926), pp. 33-36. Humorous sketch. 2,000 words.

"Moss Island," *The Quest* (Vol. 8, No. 1, May, 1930), pp. 9-14. Scientific weird. 3,700 words. Post-graduate appearance written while at the University of Minnesota. This version takes place "off the Rentharpian coast," whereas the professionally published account in *Amazing Stories Quarterly* (Winter, 1932) is located "off the New Brunswick coast."

B. *University of Minnesota*

"Mive," *Minnesota Quarterly* (Vol. VI, No. 1, Fall, 1928), pp. 16-22. Descriptive weird. 2,750 words. Later professionally published in *Weird Tales* (January, 1932). Set in "those rolling Rentharpian hills."

"The Borgian Chandelier," *Minnesota Quarterly* (Vol. VII, No. 1, Fall, 1929), pp. 61-75.

Detective. 4,700 words.

"Enter Stephen Benedict," *Minnesota Quarterly* (Vol. VII, No. 2, Winter, 1930), pp. 67-79.
Detective. 5,400 words.

"The Masked Orange," *Minnesota Quarterly* (Vol. VII, No. 3, Spring, 1930), pp. 93-101.
Detective. 3,100 words. Takes place at the shop of "Giovanni Larla—Antiques," which later figures in "Revelations in Black" (*Weird Tales,* April, 1933).

II. *Magazine Publications*

"Rumbling Cannon," *Secret Service Stories* (Vol. 2, No. 5, September, 1928), pp. 76-84.
Detective. 7,500 words. Tried at *Real Detective Tales* (rejection slip with note). Sold direct for $12.00, payable upon publication. The magazine folded and Jacobi was never paid.

"Moss Island," *Amazing Stories Quarterly* (Vol. 5, No. 1, Winter, 1932), pp. 136-140.
Scientific weird. 3,700 words. First published in *The Quest* (May, 1930). Tried at *Weird Tales* (terse letter dated 18 June 1930). Sold direct for $25.00. The protagonist is a graduate student at the "University of Rentharp."

"The Haunted Ring," *Ghost Stories* (Vol. 11, No. 4, December, 1931-January, 1932), pp. 42-48.
Weird. 4,500 words. Original title: "The Coach on the Ring" (by "James K. Vermont"). Tried at *Mystic Magazine* (letter) and *Weird Tales* (letter dated 8 September 1930). Sold direct for $90.00. Last issue of *Ghost Stories.*

"Mive," *Weird Tales* (Vol. XIX, No. 1, January, 1932) pp. 113-117.
Descriptive weird. 2,750 words. First published in *Minnesota Quarterly* (Fall, 1928). Sold direct first trip out on 27 January 1930, for $25.00, payable upon publication. Set in "those rolling Rentharpian hills."

"Revelations in Black," *Weird Tales* (Vol. 21, No. 4, April, 1933), pp. 495-509.
Weird. 9,000 words. Original title: "Larla's Volume Three" (by "Stephen Benedict"). Tried at *Strange Tales* (fine letter), *Ghost Stories* (letter asking for more), and *Weird Tales* (letter dated 6 May 1931). Revised and resubmitted to *Weird Tales* at Farnsworth Wright's request (letter dated 9 January 1932). Sold direct on second submission to *Weird Tales* on 5 March 1932, for $90.00, payable upon publication. New title furnished at Wright's request. First installment of $45.00 paid on account in July, 1933.

"The Last Drive," *Weird Tales* (Vol. 21, No. 6, June, 1933), pp. 778-781.
Weird. 2,000 words. Sold direct first trip out on 17 March 1932, for $20.00, payable upon publication. The protagonist finds himself "alone in these Rentharpian Hills."

"A Pair of Swords," *Weird Tales* (Vol. 22, No. 2, August, 1933), pp. 256-258.
Weird. 1,500 words. Tried at *Weird Tales* (letter from Farnsworth Wright dated 8 September 1932). Sold direct on second submission on 9 January 1933, for $15.00, payable upon publication.

Weird Tales
(April, 1933)

Top-Notch
(January, 1934)

"The Tomb from Beyond," *Wonder Stories* (Vol. 5, No. 4, November, 1933), pp. 355-365.

Scientific weird. 6,200 words. Original title: "Lake Macabre." Longer novelette tried at *Weird Tales* (letter from Farnsworth Wright dated 29 September 1932). Shortened from 14,000 to 11,000 words and retitled "The Lake Horror." Tried at *Amazing Stories* (rejection slip with comment, "No real science"), *Strange Tales* (letter from editor Harry Bates, calling it "too talky"), and *Weird Tales* (cordial letter from Farnsworth Wright dated 3 April 1933). Shortened from 11,000 to 6,200 words and retitled "The Geometric Tomb." Sold direct for $35.00, payable upon publication. Paid two years later, in 1935, after collection (at a charge of $10.00) was placed in the hands of a New York attorney.

"Smoke of the Snake," *Top-Notch* (Vol. XCIV, No. 1, January, 1934), pp. 63-74.

Borneo weird. 6,300 words. Tried at *Short Stories* (rejection slip), *Weird Tales* (good letter from Farnsworth Wright dated 26 June 1933), and *Dime Mystery Magazine* (note asking for more). Sold direct to Street & Smith's *Astounding Stories* for $65.00, payable upon acceptance (letter from editor Desmond Hall asking to see everything Jacobi wrote). Not weird enough for *Astounding Stories,* so published in Street & Smith's *Top-Notch.*

"The Bantam Ben Hur," *Wild West Stories and Complete Novel Magazine* (No. 105, March, 1934), pp. 119-128.

Western. 5,400 words. Tried at *Argosy* (letter), *Short Stories* (letter), *Complete Western* (rejection slip), *The Blue Book Magazine* (rejection slip), *Smoker's Magazine* (good letter), and *Nickel Western* (good letter). Sold direct on 11 November 1933, for $25.00, payable upon publication.

"The Cane," *Weird Tales* (Vol. 23, No. 4, April, 1934), pp. 502-510.

Weird. 5,000 words. Tried at *Weird Tales* (letter from Farnsworth Wright dated 30 November 1932). Sold direct on second submission on 19 January 1933, for $50.00, payable upon publication.

"Crocodile," *Complete Stories* (Vol. XXXV, No. 4, April 30, 1934), pp. 147-155.

Borneo adventure. 4,000 words. Tried at *Short Stories* (rejection slip). Sold direct on 26 December 1933, for $80.00, payable upon acceptance.

"The Satanic Piano," *Weird Tales* (Vol. 23, No. 5, May, 1934), pp. 581-600.

Weird. 12,000-word novelette. Original title: "The Death Piano." Sold direct first trip out to *Strange Tales* in 1932 for $240.00, payable upon acceptance. Manuscript returned by editor Harry Bates when *Strange Tales* ceased publication in January, 1933, after putting out seven issues. Tried at *Weird Tales* (letter from Farnsworth Wright dated 6 October 1932). Sold direct on second submission to *Weird Tales* on 27 March 1933, for $120.00, payable upon publication. First time Jacobi was paid twice for a story.

"Phantom Brass," *Railroad Stories* (Vol. XV, No. 1, August, 1934), pp. 66-71.

Railroad weird. 2,500 words. Tried at *Astounding Stories* (fine letter from editor Desmond Hall asking for a science yarn) and *Weird Tales* (letter from Farnsworth Wright dated 28 November 1933, claiming he had seen similar plot situations before). Sold direct for $35.00 (letter from editor Freeman Hubbard asking for more). Jacobi became an honorary telegrapher when his by-line called him an "Ex-Brass-Pounder."

"Jungle Wires," *Complete Stories* (Vol. XXXVI, No. 5, September 24, 1934), pp. 96-105.

Phantom Brass

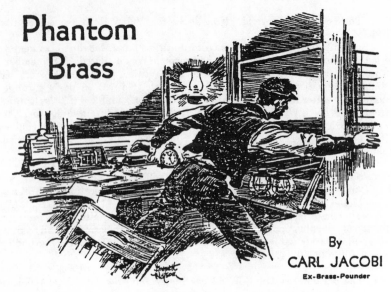

By
CARL JACOBI
Ex-Brass-Pounder

Railroad Stories
(August, 1934)

There is only one way to pay a gentleman's debt of honor—.De Horn's way.

JUNGLE WIRES

By CARL JACOBI

Complete Stories
(September 24, 1934)

Borneo adventure. 5,000 words. Sold direct first trip out for $50.00, payable upon acceptance.

"Satan's Roadhouse," *Terror Tales* (Vol. 1, No. 2, October, 1934), pp. 52-74.
Horror detective. 13,000-word novelette. Working title: "Club Macabre." Original title: "The Devil Club." Sold direct first trip out to Popular Publications' *Dime Mystery Magazine* for $130.00. Scheduled to appear in the September, 1934, issue of *Dime Mystery Magazine,* but published in Popular Publications' *Terror Tales.*

"Letter of Dismissal," *Top-Notch* (Vol. XCV, No. 4, October, 1934), pp. 87-97.
Borneo adventure. 6,500 words. Tried at *Complete Stories* (rejection slip). Sold direct on 30 July 1934, for $65.00, payable upon acceptance.

"Three Brass Cubes," *Complete Stories* (Vol. XXXVII, No. 5, January 28, 1935), pp. 114-121.
Baluchistan adventure. 4,500 words. Longer version tried at *Complete Stories* (rejection slip) and Popular Fiction Publishing Company (good letter). Sold direct to *Oriental Stories* on 27 January 1932, for $70.00, payable upon publication. After the title of the magazine was changed to *The Magic Carpet Magazine,* editor Farnsworth Wright informed Jacobi (in letters dated 7 February and 24 May 1934) that it had temporarily suspended publication. As he could not use the manuscript for at least a year, Wright returned it with the provision that he would buy it back once the magazine resumed publication, if Jacobi had not yet placed it. Revised and shortened from 7,000 to 4,500 words. Tried at *Argosy.* Sold direct on 22 October 1934, for $50.00, payable upon acceptance.

"Deceit Post," *Complete Stories,* (Vol. XXXVII, No. 6, February 18, 1935), pp. 103-114.
Borneo adventure. 6,000 words. Sold direct first trip out on 12 November 1934, for $60.00, payable upon acceptance.

"Sumpitan," *Top-Notch* (Vol. XCVII, No. 4, October, 1935), pp. 9-19.
Borneo adventure. 5,000 words. Tried at *Complete Stories* (short note) and *Adventure* (nice letter from editor Howard Bloomfield asking for more). Sold direct on 5 August 1935, for $50.00, payable upon acceptance.

"Quarry," *Dime Adventure Magazine* (Vol. 1, No. 5, December, 1935), pp. 62-69.
Borneo adventure. 4,500 words. Sold direct first trip out to Popular Publications' *Adventure* on 8 August 1935, for $45.00, payable upon publication. Scheduled to appear in *Adventure,* but published in Popular Publications' *Dime Adventure Magazine.*

"Train Kidnap," *Toronto Star Weekly,* December 21, 1935, pp. 4, 6.
Railroad adventure. 5,000 words. Original title: "Emergency." Aimed at *Railroad Stories.* Tried at *Railroad Stories* (letter stating the plot was too old), *Top-Notch* (short note from editor F. Orlin Tremaine), and *Short Stories.* Sold by agent Otis Adelbert Kline to this Canadian newspaper for $35.00, payable upon publication. Jacobi received payment on 15 January 1936.

"Loaded Coupling," *Maclean's Magazine,* (Vol. 49, No. 3, February 1, 1936), pp. 16-17, 39-40, 42.
Railroad adventure. 6,000 words. Original title: "Brass Hands." Longer version tried at *Railroad Stories* (rejection slip with note), *Argosy* (terse note), *Short Stories* (rejection slip), and *Worker's Fiction Magazine.* Revised according to Hugh B. Cave's

suggestions, shortened from 7,200 to 6,000 words and retitled "Loaded Coupling." Tried at *Complete Stories* (letter from editor E. C. Richards stating it was usable but the magazine was filled up), *Railroad Stories* (good letter indicating they had a story with a similar plot), *Top-Notch* (letter stating the magazine was filled up), *Short Stories* (rejection slip), and, submitted by agent Otis Adelbert Kline, *Doc Savage* (fine letter asking Jacobi to study the magazine and send more). Sold by Kline to this Toronto magazine for $100.000, payable upon publication. Jacobi received payment on 15 January 1936. His first "slick" appearance.

"The Face in the Wind," *Weird Tales* (Vol. 27, No. 4, April, 1936), pp. 404-418.
Weird. 8,000 words. Original title: "Celaeno." Tried at *Astounding Stories* (rejection slip) and *Weird Tales* (letters dated 3 October and 22 November 1933). Sold direct on third submission to *Weird Tales* on 6 June 1934, for $80.00, payable upon publication. New title furnished at Farnsworth Wright's request. First installment of $40.00 paid on account on 1 September 1936. Second installment of $40.00 paid on 1 October 1936.

"Death Rides the Plateau," *Thrilling Mystery* (Vol. III, No. 1, May, 1936), pp. 80-91, 119-121.
Terror. 8,000-word novelette. Agent Lurton Blassingame and editor-in-chief Leo Margulies of the Thrilling Publication chain cooked up the plot and sent it to Jacobi. Sold first trip out by Blassingame for $80.00, payable upon acceptance, of which Jacobi received $72.00. Beneath his by-line, Jacobi was credited as the author of two stories: "Bodies Without Heads," a fictitious title invented as a joke by Margulies; and "Dead Man's River," which appeared eight months later in *Thrilling Adventures*.

"Black Passage," *Thrilling Adventures* (Vol. XVII, No. 3, May, 1936), pp. 90-102.
Sea adventure. 7,500-word novelette. Tried at *Top-Notch* (short note) and *All-Star Adventure Fiction* (short note asking for more). Sold by agent Lurton Blassingame for $75.00, payable upon acceptance, of which Jacobi received $67.50. Editor-in-chief Leo Margulies, up to his old tricks, supplied two more fictitious titles beneath Jacobi's by-line: "Tide of Terror" and "Beach of Death."

"Ticket to Nowhere," *Airlanes* (Vol. 1, No. 3, May, 1936), pp. 14-15.
Domestic. 1,500-word short-short. Tried at *Liberty* (rejection slip). Sold by agent Otis Adelbert Kline for $18.00, payable upon publication, of which Jacobi was to have received $16.20. Two years later, $10.00 had been paid, with $8.00 outstanding. Complimentary magazine given to airline passengers. Jacobi's second "slick" appearance.

"Spider Wires," *Thrilling Adventures* (Vol. XX, No. 2, January, 1937), pp. 47-53, 68.
Borneo adventure. 4,700 words. Sold first trip out by agent Lurton Blassingame for $50.00, payable upon acceptance, of which Jacobi received $45.00 on 28 September 1936. Jacobi's only appearance under a pseudonym (Jackson Cole); used because "Dead Man's River" appeared in the same issue under his own by-line.

"Dead Man's River," *Thrilling Adventures* (Vol. XX, No. 2, January, 1937), pp. 100-108.
Borneo adventure. 5,200 words. Sold first trip out by agent Lurton Blassingame on 18 May 1936, for $50.00, payable upon acceptance, of which Jacobi received $45.00. Jacobi's "Spider Wires" also appeared in this issue under the house pseudonym, Jackson Cole.

There's
Dynamite
Wrapped
In Parchment
When a Man
Is Tempted!

Letter of DISMISSAL
By CARL JACOBI

"You're slippery, all right," Mueller said, "but I'm putting you out of my way right now!"

I WAS NEAR nightfall when Lieutenant Henston reached the mouth of the Boh River. Six days from the Long Nawang garrison through Dutch Borneo's most dangerous headhunting region had been passed without trouble. Ahead was the Mahakam, an almost-unbroken route to the coast.

But Henston, as he strode down the swamp trail toward the nameless Dyak village that lay a quarter of a mile inland, showed no signs of relief. Coming into the Mahakam completed but the first stage of his hazardous journey. Anything could happen before he reached military headquarters at

"The World in a Box," *Thrilling Wonder Stories* (Vol. 9, No. 1, February, 1937), pp. 103-113.
Science fiction. 6,600 words. Written in 1928. Tried at *Astounding Stories* (rejection slip), *Weird Tales* (letter from Farnsworth Wright dated 24 May 1934, calling it "trite"), and, submitted by agent Otis Adelbert Kline, *Weird Tales* (Wright still found it unconvincing). Kline returned the manuscript after trying all available markets, but later sold it, on 11 April 1936, for $66.00, payable upon acceptance, of which Jacobi received $56.10. Hugo Gernsback's *Wonder Stories* had been purchased by Standard Publications, and became *Thrilling Wonder Stories*.

"Tiger Island," *Thrilling Adventures* (Vol. XXI, No. 3, May, 1937), pp. 65-72.
Sea adventure. 4,800 words. Working title: "Pearls Below." Tried at *Complete Stories* (short letter), *Short Stories* (rejection slip), *Argosy* (short note), *Dime Adventure Magazine* (rejection slip), *Top-Notch* (short note), and *Doc Savage* (good letter). Sold by agent Otis Adelbert Kline on 16 October 1936, for $50.00, payable upon acceptance, of which Jacobi received $42.50.

"Satan's Kite," *Thrilling Mystery* (Vol. VII, No. 3, June, 1937), pp. 68-73.
Borneo weird. 3,500 words. Original title: "The Kite." Longer version tried at *Weird Tales* (letter from Farnsworth Wright dated 8 September 1934, claiming it was neither up to standard nor all that clear). Jacobi agreed, but resubmitted to *Weird Tales* (in letters dated 22 May 1935 and 15 May 1936, Wright still found it unconvincing). Sent to agent Otis Adelbert Kline, who returned the manuscript (no market except *Weird Tales*). Revised (injecting the terror angle), tightened, shortened from 6,500 to 3,500 words, and retitled "Satan's Kite." Sold by agent Lurton Blassingame on 18 February 1937, for $35.00, payable upon acceptance, of which Jacobi received $31.50.

"East of Samarinda," *The Skipper* (Vol. II, No. 2, July, 1937), pp. 86-101.
Borneo adventure. 10,000-word novelette. Longer version revised and shortened from 15,000 to 10,000 words. Sold first trip out by agent Lurton Blassingame to Street & Smith's *Doc Savage* on 1 February 1937, for $100.00, payable upon acceptance, of which Jacobi received $90.00. Scheduled to appear in *Doc Savage,* but published in Street & Smith's *The Skipper.*

"Balu Guns," *Thrilling Adventures* (Vol. XXIII, No. 1, September, 1937), pp. 45-55.
Baluchistan adventure. 6,000 words. Working title: "Juloh." Original title: "Dogs of the Wind." Alternate title: "The Balu Break." Longer novelette tried at *Oriental Stories* (letters dated 9 June and 30 August 1932), *Argosy* (terse note, then good letter asking for more), *Thrilling Adventures* (rejection slip), *Danger Trail* (not even a rejection slip, then rejection slip), *Top-Notch* (rejection slip), *World Adventurer* (rejection slip), and, submitted by agent Otis Adelbert Kline, *Thrilling Adventures* (letter stating it lacked punch). Revised, shortened from 15,000 to 6,000 words, and retitled "Balu Guns." Sold by Kline on 4 March 1937, for $60.00, payable upon acceptance, of which Jacobi received $51.00.

"A Film in the Bush," *Doc Savage* (Vol. X, No. 1, September, 1937), pp. 105-112.
Borneo adventure. 4,200 words. Similar to earlier yarns, rather hastily written, and aimed at *Doc Savage.* Sold first trip out by agent Lurton Blassingame to Street & Smith's *The Skipper* on 21 June 1937, for $42.00, payable upon acceptance, of which Jacobi received $37.80. Scheduled to appear in *The Skipper,* but published in Street & Smith's *Doc Savage.*

"Wings for a Monster," *The Phantom Detective* (Vol. XX, No. 3, October, 1937), pp. 93-100.

Weird detective. 4,500 words. Original title: "Winged Menace." Hastily written and aimed at *Doctor Death*. Agent Otis Adelbert Kline returned the manuscript after trying all available markets. Retitled "Wings for a Monster." Sold by agent Lurton Blassingame on 5 May 1937, for $45.00, payable upon acceptance, of which Jacobi received $40.50.

"Head in His Hands," *Thrilling Mystery* (Vol. VIII, No. 3, November, 1937), pp. 56-63.

Terror mystery. 4,500 words. Aimed at *Thrilling Mystery*. Sold first trip out by agent Lurton Blassingame on 22 March 1937, for $50.00, payable upon acceptance, of which Jacobi received $45.00.

"Death On Tin Can," *The Skipper* (Vol. II, No. 6, December, 1937), pp. 112-122.

Sea adventure. 6,000 words. Original title: "Black Pearl." Alternate title: "Tin Can Island." Tried by agent Lurton Blassingame at *Argosy* and *Top-Notch*. Retitled "Death On Tin Can." Sold by Blassingame on 26 July 1937, for $60.00, payable upon acceptance, of which Jacobi received $54.00. Last issue of *The Skipper*, which was combined the following month with another Street & Smith publication, *Doc Savage*.

"The Bells Toll Blood," *Thrilling Mystery* (Vol. IX, No. 1, January, 1938), pp. 100-111.

Terror. 5,000 words. Aimed at Popular Publications (*Dime Mystery Magazine* or *Terror Tales*). Longer novelette tried at Popular Publications (letter from editor Rogers Terrill stating it was too gory and lacked sufficient menace). Shortened from 11,000 to 5,000 words. Sold by agent Lurton Blassingame on 12 May 1937, for $50.00, payable upon acceptance, of which Jacobi received $45.00.

"Holt Sails the 'San Hing'," *Short Stories* (Vol. CLXII, No. 2, January 25, 1938), pp. 124-134.

Sea adventure. 6,700 words. Working title: "Murder Cruise." Original title: "Death Sails the San Hing." Agent Lurton Blassingame returned the manuscript for revision. Retitled "Holt Sails the San Hing." Sold first trip out by Blassingame on 18 October 1937, for $60.00, payable upon acceptance, of which Jacobi received $54.00 on 6 December 1937.

"The Devil Deals," *Weird Tales* (Vol. 31, No. 4, April, 1938), pp. 387-392.

Weird. 3,000 words. Original title: "The King and the Knave." Longer version tried at *Weird Tales* (letter from Farnsworth Wright dated 5 May 1936, indicating he found it unconvincing). Shortened from 5,000 to 3,000 words, retitled "The Devil Deals," and aimed at *Thrilling Mystery*. Sold on second submission by agent Lurton Blassingame on 12 May 1937, for $30.00, payable upon publication, of which Jacobi received $27.00 on 3 March 1938.

"Leopard Tracks," *Short Stories* (Vol. CLXIV, No. 1, July 10, 1938), pp. 122-135.

Borneo adventure. 8,000-word novelette. Tried by agent Lurton Blassingame at *Thrilling Adventures* (letter from editor Leo Margulies stating the plot was old and it was just a fair yarn). Blassingame requested that several pages be revised, and Jacobi assumed it would not sell. Sold by Blassingame on 20 January 1938, for $80.00, payable upon acceptance, of which Jacobi received $72.00 on 1 February 1938.

"House of the Ravens," *Thrilling Mystery* (Vol. X, No. 2, September, 1938), pp. 44-56.

Terror detective. 7,500-word novelette. Original title: "House of the Corbies." Sold first trip out by agent Lurton Blassingame on 14 March 1938, for $75.00, payable upon acceptance, of which Jacobi received $67.50. Set in the "bleak Rentharpian hills."

"Cosmic Teletype," *Thrilling Wonder Stories* (Vol. XII, No. 2, October, 1938), pp. 35-43.
  Science fiction. 5,000 words. Shorter version tried by agent Lurton Blassingame at *Thrilling Wonder Stories* (note from editor Leo Margulies requesting revision of the ending). Revised and expanded from 3,800 to 5,000 words. Sold on second submission by Blassingame on 16 May 1938, for $50.00, payable upon acceptance, of which Jacobi received $45.00.

"Murder for Medusa," *Thrilling Mystery* (Vol. XI, No. 1, January, 1939), pp. 94-101, 108-113.
  Terror detective. 6,500 words. Shorter version tried by agent Lurton Blassingame at *Thrilling Mystery* (letter from editor Leo Margulies requesting revision). Revised according to Margulies' suggestions and expanded from 6,000 to 6,500 words. Sold on second submission by Blassingame on 3 March 1938, for $65.00, payable upon acceptance, of which Jacobi received $58.50.

"The War of the Weeds," *Thrilling Wonder Stories* (Vol. XIII, No. 1, February, 1939), pp. 41-49.
  Science fiction. 5,600 words. Aimed at *Thrilling Wonder Stories*. Sold first trip out by agent Lurton Blassingame on 5 October 1938, for $56.00, payable upon acceptance, of which Jacobi received $47.00.

"Drowned Destiny," *12 Adventure Stories* (Vol. I, No. not known, March, 1939), pp. not known.
  Terror. 6,000 words. Original title: "Hell on the Bottom." Aimed at *Thrilling Mystery*. Retitled "Drowned Destiny" by agent Lurton Blassingame. Tried by Blassingame at *Thrilling Mystery*. Sold by Blassingame for $30.00, payable upon publication, of which Jacobi received $27.00 on 1 March 1939. (The author has been unable to locate this issue; nor has he been able to read the story in manuscript, as it is non-extant.)

"Death's Outpost," *Thrilling Mystery* (Vol. XI, No. 3, May, 1939), pp. 86-94.
  New Guinea terror. 5,300 words. Aimed at *Thrilling Mystery*. Sold first trip out by agent Lurton Blassingame on 19 December 1938, for $53.00, payable upon acceptance, of which Jacobi received $47.70.

"Flight of the Flame Fiend," *Thrilling Mystery* (Vol. XII, No. 1, July, 1939), pp. 13-28.
  Terror mystery. 9,000-word novelette. Aimed at *Thrilling Mystery*. Sold first trip out by agent Lurton Blassingame on 15 September 1938, for $90.00, payable upon acceptance, of which Jacobi received $81.00.

"Sagasta's Last," *Strange Stories* (Vol. II, No. 1, August, 1939), pp. 67-71, 76.
  Weird. 3,300 words. Original title: "Through the Glass." Sent to agent Lurton Blassingame. Tried direct at *Weird Tales* (letter dated 29 October 1936). New title suggested by August Derleth. Sold direct on 11 March 1939, for $15.00.

"Trial by Jungle," *Thrilling Adventures* (Vol. XXXI, No. 1, September, 1939), pp. 83-91, 104.

Borneo adventure. 5,000 words. Original title: "Gentleman from Borneo." Revised at the request of agent Lurton Blassingame. Blassingame returned the manuscript on 12 December 1938, after trying all available markets. Tried at *Adventure*. Retitled "Trial by Jungle." Sold direct for $50.00, payable upon acceptance.

"Spawn of Blackness," *Strange Stories* (Vol. II, No. 2, October, 1939), pp. 112-118, 120-122.
Weird. 5,900 words. Original title: "The Color Fiend." Longer novelette tried at *Weird Tales* (letter dated 10 November 1933) and *Astounding Science-Fiction* (fine letter from editor Desmond Hall in 1938, praising Jacobi's writing, asking for more, and explaining that the magazine had changed its policy to straight science fiction). Revised (switching the setting from London to America), shortened from 8,000 to 5,900 words, and retitled "Spawn of Blackness." Tried at *Dime Detective Magazine* (fine letter from editor Rogers Terrill asking for more), *Strange Detective Stories* (good letter), *Ten Detective Aces* (letter asking for more), and *Super-Detective* (rejection slip with note that the editor liked its style but it lacked action). Sold direct on 11 March 1939, for $30.00.

"The Twenty-One Crescents," *Thrilling Adventures* (Vol. XXXI, No. 3, November, 1939), pp. 54-73.
Baluchistan adventure. 10,000-word novelette. Aimed at *Thrilling Adventures*. Sold first trip out by agent Lurton Blassingame for $50.00, payable upon acceptance, of which Jacobi received $45.00. He also got his first cover illustration.

"Sky Trap," *Science Fiction* (Vol. 1, No. 6, March, 1940), pp. 69-84.
Science fiction. 9,500-word novelette. Original title: "Sky Sargasso." Tried at *Astounding Stories* (fine letter from editor Desmond Hall in 1934, asking for more and stating it had also been considered for *Top Notch*), *Argosy* (terse note from editor Don Moore stating it had too much science and not enough plot), and *Weird Tales* (letter from Farnsworth Wright dated 13 February 1936, commenting that it was not a "weird"). Sold by agent Otis Adelbert Kline for $50.00, payable upon publication, of which Jacobi received $42.50 on 8 April 1940.

"Laughter in the Wind," *Thrilling Mystery* (Vol. XIV, No. 3, May, 1940), pp. 39-47.
Terror mystery. 5,000 words. Sold first trip out by agent Lurton Blassingame on 25 January 1940, for $50.00, payable upon acceptance, of which Jacobi received $45.00.

"Captain Jinx," *Red Star Adventures* (Vol. 1, No. 2, August, 1940), pp. 70-87.
Sea adventure. 9,000-word novelette. Original title: "Heliotrope Cruise." Sold first trip out by agent Lurton Blassingame to Munsey's *Argosy* for $90.00, payable upon acceptance, of which Jacobi received $81.00 on 1 April 1940. Scheduled to appear in *Argosy*, but published in Munsey's *Red Star Adventures*.

"The Phantom Pistol," *Weird Tales* (Vol. 35, No. 9, May, 1941), pp. 62-70.
Weird. 5,000 words. Original title: "The Curse Pistol." Longer novelette sold direct first trip out to *Strange Tales* in 1932 for $160.00, payable upon acceptance, but remained unpublished when the magazine folded in January, 1933, after putting out seven issues. Shortened from 8,000 to 5,000 words and retitled "The Phantom Pistol." Sold by agent Lurton Blassingame in November, 1939, for $50.00, payable upon publication, of which Jacobi received $45.00 on 8 January 1941 (prior to publication). Second time Jacobi was paid twice for a story.

"The Face in the Wind" (*Weird Tales,* April, 1936);
illustration by Virgil Finlay

The Devil Deals

By CARL JACOBI

Weird Tales (April, 1938); heading by Virgil Finlay

"The Street That Wasn't There," *Comet* (Vol. 1, No. 5, July, 1941), pp. 18-27.

Science fantasy. 5,600 words. Collaboration between Clifford D. Simak and Jacobi. Aimed at *Unknown*. Tried at *Unknown* (letter from editor John W. Campbell, Jr.). Sold direct for $56.00, payable upon publication. The magazine folded and defaulted on payment. The Authors' Guild effected a forty-percent settlement of $22.00, of which each author received $11.00 in the fall of 1941.

"Redemption Trail," *Thrilling Adventures* (Vol. XXXIX, No. 1, October, 1941), pp. 85-94.

Borneo adventure. 5,000 words. Aimed at *Argosy*. Sold first trip out by agent Lurton Blassingame on 1 March 1941, for $50.00, payable upon acceptance, of which Jacobi received $45.00.

"Hamadryad Chair," *10 Story Mystery Magazine* (Vol. 1, No. 2, February, 1942), pp. 25-32.

Borneo terror. 5,000 words. Original title: "The Palapak Chair." Aimed at *Argosy* or *Adventure*. Tried by agent Otis Adelbert Kline at *Argosy* (letter from editor Can Whipple in 1937, claiming the ending was weak). Revised (injecting the terror angle), retitled "Hamadryad Chair," and aimed at *Thrilling Mystery* in 1941. Tried by agent Lurton Blassingame at *Thrilling Mystery*. Sold by Blassingame for $25.00, of which Jacobi received $22.50.

"Cosmic Castaway," *Planet Stories* (Vol. II, No. 2, March, 1943), pp. 2-23.

Science fiction. 15,000-word novelette. Working title: "Crusoe of Space." Original title: "The Space Hawk." Longer version tried at *Thrilling Wonder Stories* (letter from editor Leo Margulies dated 12 August 1939). Revised and shortened from 20,000 to 15,000 words. Sold by agent Lurton Blassingtame in April, 1942, for $150.00, payable upon acceptance, of which Jacobi received $135.00.

"Assignment on Venus," *Planet Stories* (Vol. II, No. 4, Fall, 1943), pp. 73-80.

Science fiction. 5,000 words. Working title: "Dismissal on Venus." Original title: "Dismissal Cylinder." Aimed at *Planet Stories*. Sold first trip out by agent Lurton Blassingame in October, 1942, for $50.00, payable upon acceptance, of which Jacobi received $45.00. Reworking of an old Borneo yarn, "Letter of Dismissal" (*Top-Notch*, October, 1934).

"Black Lace," *Thrilling Adventures* (Vol. XLVI, No. 1, November, 1943), pp. 52-65.

Costume adventure. 8,000-word novelette. Longer weird version aimed at *Weird Tales*. Tried by agent Lurton Blassingame at *Weird Tales* (letter from Farnsworth Wright dated 27 April 1938, claiming it was more an adventure than a "weird") and *Strange Stories* (letter from editor Leo Margulies stating that the eerie element was just thrown in). Rewritten as a straight pirate yarn and shortened from 10,000 to 8,000 words. Sold by Blassingame in February, 1943, for $80.00, payable upon acceptance, of which Jacobi received $72.00.

"Submarine I-26," *Doc Savage* (Vol. XXIII, No. 1, March, 1944), pp. 81-93.

Borneo war adventure. 6,000 words. Original title: "I-26." Longer novelette tried by agent Lurton Blassingame at *Argosy, Short Stories,* and *Doc Savage* (letter from editor Charles Moran requesting revision). Revised and shortened from 8,000 to 6,000 words. Sold by Blassingame on 2 December 1943, for $60.00, payable upon acceptance, of which Jacobi received $54.00.

Spawn of Blackness

An Evil God Shuns the Light and Seeks Victims in Darkness!

By CARL JACOBI

*Author of "House of the Ravens,"
"Cosmic Teletype," etc.*

IT LACKED twenty minutes of midnight when I locked the door of my apartment and raced down the steps to the waiting cab. A heavy rain, driven by a howling wind, swirled across the pavement.

"Sixteen Monroe Street," I snapped to the driver. "Oak Square. And drive like hell!"

The cab jerked forward, roared north into Monte Curve and turned east toward Carter. I leaned back then and prayed for a clear way through the night traffic. But even with the best of luck I knew I was treading on counted time.

Only a scant few minutes before, I had been in bed asleep. Then had come that urgent telephone call with that familiar voice over the wire.

"Dr. Haxton? Dr. James Haxton? This is your old friend, Stephen Fay. Can you come immediately? Something terrible has happened, and I'm in need of medical help. Hurry, man!"

It stood there a moment, eyes blinking in the sudden glare

"Canal," *Startling Stories* (Vol. 10, No. 3, Spring, 1944), pp. 78-87.

Science fantasy. 5,500 words. Aimed at *Astounding Science-Fiction.* Tried by agent Lurton Blassingame at *Astounding Science-Fiction* (letter from editor John W. Campbell, Jr.). Sold by Blassingame to Better Publications on 28 March 1943, for $55.00, payable upon acceptance, of which Jacobi received $49.50. Scheduled to appear in *Thrilling Wonder Stories,* but published in *Startling Stories.* Reworking of an old Borneo yarn, "Quarry" (*Dime Adventure Magazine,* December, 1935).

"The Cosmic Doodler," *Startling Stories* (Vol. 11, No. 2, Fall, 1944), pp. 65-73.

Science fantasy. 5,000 words. Original title: "Space Scribblers." Tried at *Astounding Science-Fiction* (short letter from editor John W. Campbell, Jr., in 1939, saying the writing was good but the idea was not strong enough to carry the story), *Amazing Stories,* and, submitted by agent Lurton Blassingame, *Thrilling Wonder Stories.* Revised and retitled "The Cosmic Doodler." Sold direct to Better Publications for $50.00, payable upon acceptance. Scheduled to appear in *Thrilling Wonder Stories,* but published in *Startling Stories.*

"Doctor Universe," *Planet Stories* (Vol. II, No. 8, Fall, 1944), pp. 35-44.

Science fiction. 6,000 words. Original title: "The Bells of Dr. Universe." Aimed at *Planet Stories.* Longer novelette sent to agent Lurton Blassingame, who returned the manuscript. Revised, shortened from 8,000 to 6,000 words, and retitled "Lady of the Green Flames." Sold direct first trip out on 11 December 1943, for $60.00, payable upon acceptance.

"Double Trouble," *Planet Stories* (Vol. II, No. 10, Spring Issue, December-February, 1944-1945), pp. 69-76.

Science fiction. 5,500 words. Sequel to "Doctor Universe" (*Planet Stories,* Fall, 1944). Original title: "Lady of the Silver Cockatoos." Aimed at *Planet Stories.* Sold direct first trip out on 20 March 1944, for $55.00, payable upon acceptance.

"Carnaby's Fish," *Weird Tales* (Vol. 38, No. 6, July, 1945), pp. 74-80.

Weird. 5,000 words. Tried at *Weird Tales* (letter from Dorothy McIlwraith) and *Unknown Worlds* (letter from editor John W. Campbell, Jr., dated 23 August 1943). Revised according to August Derleth's suggestions. Sold direct on second submission to *Weird Tales* in 1945, for $50.00, payable upon publication.

"Enter the Nebula," *Planet Stories* (Vol. III, No. 4, Fall Issue, June-August, 1946), pp. 34-48.

Science fiction. 10,000-word novelette. Working title: "The Blue Star Figurines." Aimed at *Planet Stories.* Tried at *Planet Stories* (letter from editor W. Scott Peacock requesting revision). Revised. Sold direct on second submission on 25 September 1944, for $100.00, payable upon acceptance.

"Tepondicon," *Planet Stories* (Vol. III, No. 5, Winter Issue, September-November, 1946), pp. 40-47.

Science fiction. 5,000 words. Aimed at *Planet Stories.* Sold direct first trip out on 16 July 1945, for $50.00, payable upon acceptance.

"The Corbie Door," *Weird Tales* (Vol. 39, No. 11, May, 1947), pp. 55-67.

Weird. 9,000-word novelette. Aimed at *Weird Tales.* Revised according to August Derleth's suggestions and expanded from 5,000 to 9,000 words. After reading the revised version, Derleth sent a letter praising it to Lamont Buchanan, associate editor of *Weird Tales.* Sold direct first trip out in November, 1946, for $90.00, payable upon publication.

Challenging, forbidding, waited the
dread guest chair of Kayan Plantation—
the chair whose touch meant death!

10 Story Mystery Magazine (February, 1942)

"The Digging at Pistol Key," *Weird Tales* (Vol. 39, No. 11, July, 1947), pp. 86-95.
Weird. 5,000 words. Aimed at *Weird Tales*. Revised according to August Derleth's suggestions. Sold direct first trip out on 3 March 1947, for $50.00 (check from associate editor Lamont Buchanan enclosed with letter of acceptance). Note that the *Weird Tales* issues for May and July, 1947, were inadvertently given the same number.

"Lodana," *Startling Stories,* (Vol. 16, No. 1, September, 1947), pp. 80-86, 95.
Science fiction. 5,000 words. Aimed at *Thrilling Wonder Stories.* Sold direct first trip out to Better Publications on 11 August 1946, for $75.00, payable upon acceptance. Scheduled to appear in *Thrilling Wonder Stories,* but published in *Startling Stories.*

"Portrait in Moonlight," *Weird Tales* (Vol. 40, No. 1, November, 1947), pp. 66-73.
Weird. 5,000 words. Working title: "Portrait in the Moonlight." Aimed at *Weird Tales.* Title shortened at August Derleth's suggestion. Sold direct first trip out on 5 May 1947, for $50.00.

"The Random Quantity," *Avon Fantasy Reader No. 5,* ed. Donald A. Wollheim (New York: Avon Book Company, 1947), pp. 54-61.
Weird. 3,000 words. Longer version tried at *Ellery Queen's Mystery Magazine* (fine letter asking for more), *Weird Tales* (short note), and *Esquire* (rejection slip with note saying the pseudo-science was unconvincing). Shortened from 4,500 to 3,000 words. Sold direct for $60.00. Saddle-stitched, digest-sized magazine in paperback format.

"The Lorenzo Watch," *Weird Tales* (Vol. 40, No. 2, January, 1948), pp. 85-94.
Weird. 5,000 words. Revised according to August Derleth's suggestions. Tried at *Avon Fantasy Reader.* Sold direct for $50.00.

"The La Prello Paper," *Weird Tales* (Vol. 40, No. 3, March, 1948), pp. 38-43.
Weird. 4,500 words. Working title: "Micomicon." Aimed at *Weird Tales.* Sold direct first trip out in October, 1947, for $45.00. *Weird Tales'* 25th-anniversary issue.

"Gentlemen, the Scavengers!," *Thrilling Wonder Stories* (Vol. XXXII, No. 1, April, 1948), pp. 80-87.
Science fiction. 5,000 words. Sold direct first trip out in March, 1947, for $75.00, payable upon acceptance.

"The Jade Scarlotti," *Short Stories* (Vol. CCV, No. 1, July 10, 1948), pp. 119-127.
Borneo sea adventure. 5,000 words. Tried at *The Blue Book Magazine* (brief letter). Sold direct in April, 1948, for $65.00, payable upon acceptance.

"Incident at the Galloping Horse," *Weird Tales* (Vol. 41, No. 1, November, 1948), pp. 47-55.
Weird. 5,000 words. Aimed at *Weird Tales.* Sold direct first trip out in July, 1948, for $50.00.

"Matthew South and Company," *Weird Tales* (Vol. 41, No. 4, May, 1949), pp. 22-30.
Weird. 5,000 words. Aimed at *Weird Tales.* Sold direct first trip out on 3 November 1948, for $50.00.

"Her Impulse Day," *Star Weekly,* May 21, 1949, pp. 1, 4 (magazine section).
Romance. 5,000 words. Tried at *Ladies' Home Journal* (nice letter), *Woman's*

Home Companion (brief letter), and *Maclean's Magazine* (brief letter dated 1 November 1948). Sold direct in December, 1948, for $300.00, of which Jacobi received $255.00 after fifteen-percent Canadian copyright tax was deducted. Appeared in the magazine section of this Toronto newspaper. In Port-of-Spain, Trinidad, the protagonist meets one Jose Sagasta, whose name Jacobi had used in "Sagasta's Last" (*Strange Stories*, August, 1939).

"Her Impulse Day," *New Zealand Woman's Weekly,* July 21, 1949, pp. 14-16, 32.
Romance. 5,000 words. First published in *Star Weekly* (May 21, 1949). Sold for reprint by *Star Weekly* to this Auckland newspaper. The amount Jacobi received is not known.

"The Historian," *Startling Stories* (Vol. 21, No. 2, May, 1950), pp. 137-139.
Science fiction. 1,100-word short-short. Aimed at *Thrilling Wonder Stories*. Sold direct first trip out to Standard Magazines in November, 1949, for $15.00, payable upon acceptance. Scheduled to appear in *Thrilling Wonder Stories*, but published in Better Publications' *Startling Stories*.

"The Spanish Camera," *Weird Tales* (Vol. 42, No. 6, September, 1950), pp. 70-78.
Weird. 5,000 words. Aimed at *Weird Tales*. Sold direct first trip out on 26 January 1950, for $50.00.

"The Street That Wasn't There," *Avon Fantasy Reader No. 13,* ed. Donald A. Wollheim (New York: Avon Novels, Inc., 1950), pp. 116-126.
Science fantasy. 5,600 words. Collaboration between Clifford D. Simak and Jacobi. First published in *Comet* (July, 1941). Sold for reprint for $25.00, of which each author received $12.50. Saddle-stitched, digest-sized magazine in paperback format.

"The War of the Weeds," *Fantastic Story Magazine* (Vol. 5, No. 2, March, 1953), pp. 128-136.
Science fiction. 5,600 words. First published in *Thrilling Wonder Stories* (February, 1939). Sold for reprint by agent Scott Meredith for $15.00, of which Jacobi received $13.50.

"The Gentleman Is an Epwa," *Cosmos Science Fiction and Fantasy* (Vol. 1, No. 2, November, 1953), pp. 44-58.
Science fiction. 5,500 words. First published in August Derleth's anthology, *Worlds of Tomorrow* (1953). Sold for reprint by agent Scott Meredith for $55.00, of which Jacobi received $49.50.

"Made in Tanganyika," *Fantastic Universe* (Vol. 1, No. 6, May, 1954), pp. 95-105.
Science fantasy. 5,000 words. Original title: "The Tanganyika TV." Rewritten according to August Derleth's suggestions. Sold first trip out by agent Scott Meredith in October, 1953, for $50.00, of which Jacobi received $45.00.

"The Dangerous Scarecrow," *Imagination* (Vol. 5, No. 8, August, 1954), pp. 68-76.
Weird. 3,000 words. Original title: "Witches in the Cornfield." Aimed at *Weird Tales*. Sold first trip out by agent Scott Meredith for $30.00, of which Jacobi received $27.00. Photograph of Jacobi and autobiographical sketch appear on pp. 2, 76-77.

"Strangers to Straba," *Fantastic Universe* (Vol. 2, No. 3, October, 1954), pp. 90-98.
Science fiction. 4,000 words. Working titles: "The Love Ship" and "Barlow's Narrative." Revised according to agent Scott Meredith's suggestions. Sold first trip

The Corbie Door

BY CARL JACOBI

Weird Tales (May, 1947)

out by Meredith for $40.00, of which Jacobi received $36.00.

"The Long Voyage," *Fantastic Universe* (Vol. 4, No. 2, September, 1955), pp. 38-51.
Science fiction. 7,000 words. Original title: "Long Voyage." Written in 1948 at the request of Sam Merwin, Jr., editor of *Thrilling Wonder Stories.* Tried at *Thrilling Wonder Stories* (nice letter). Revised. Tried at *Planet Stories* (rejection slip) and *Super-Science Fiction* (rejection slip). Sold by agent Scott Meredith for $70.00, of which Jacobi received $63.00.

"The Martian Calendar," *Space Science Fiction Magazine* (Vol. 1, No. 1, Spring, 1957), pp. 2-13.
Science fiction. 3,500 words. Working title: "A Day in His Life." Revised according to August Derleth's suggestions. Sold first trip out by agent Scott Meredith for $50.00, of which Jacobi received $45.00.

"The Legation Cigar," *The Saint Detective Magazine* (Vol. 8, No. 2, August, 1957), pp. 102-110.
Detective. 2,500 words. Tried at *Ellery Queen's Mystery Magazine* in 1948. Revised in 1956. Sold by agent Scott Meredith for $40.00, of which Jacobi received $36.00.

"The Commission of Captain Lace," *Short Stories Magazine* (Vol. 220, No. 2, April, 1958), pp. 79-92.
Costume adventure. 5,000 words. Sequel to "Black Lace" *(Thrilling Adventures,* November, 1943). Original title: "A Letter of Marque." Written in 1943. Agent Lurton Blassingame returned the manuscript after trying all available markets. Tried at *Maclean's Magazine* (nice letter asking for more) and *The Blue Book Magazine.* Rewritten and retitled "The Commission of Captain Lace" in 1948. Tried at *Adventure* (fine note asking for more), *The Blue Book Magazine* (rejection slip), *Short Stories* (brief note stating it did not fit in), and Toronto's *Star Weekly* (brief letter from editor Gwen Cowley saying she did not care for it). Sent to agent Scott Meredith, who returned the manuscript, in 1956. Tried at *Short Stories Magazine* (letter from editor Cylvia Kleinman in 1956). Sold direct on second submission to *Short Stories Magazine* on 18 December 1957, for $50.00, payable upon acceptance. Jacobi's second cover illustration.

"The Legation Cigar," *The Saint Detective Magazine* (Vol. 4, No. 10, August, 1958), pp. not known.
Detective. 2,500 words. First published in *The Saint Detective Magazine* (August, 1957). Jacobi was not paid for this reprint in the British edition of the same magazine.

"Moss Island," *Amazing Stories* (Vol. 40, No. 4, February, 1966), pp. 132-141.
Scientific weird. 3,700 words. First published in *The Quest* (May, 1930) and *Amazing Stories Quarterly* (Winter, 1932). Sold for reprint for $25.00, payable upon publication.

"He Looked Back," *If* (Vol. 16, No. 8, August, 1966), pp. 114-123.
Science fiction. 5,000 words. Original title: "Exit Mr. Smith." Sold first trip out by agent Scott Meredith for $75.00, of which Jacobi received $67.50.

"The Keys of Kai," *The Saint Magazine* (Vol. 25, No. 2, May, 1967), pp. 152-160.
Detective. 3,000 words. Original title: "Five White Men." Written as a Borneo adventure in 1934. Longer version tried at *Top-Notch* in April, 1935. Revised and shortened from 5,400 to 4,500 words. Sent to agent Otis Adelbert Kline, who returned

the manuscript. Rewritten as a detective yarn, shortened from 4,500 to 3,000 words, and retitled "The Case of the Java Moons" in 1957. Sent to agent Scott Meredith, who returned the manuscript. Tried at *The Saint Detective Magazine, Ellery Queen's Mystery Magazine,* and *Mike Shayne Mystery Magazine* in 1958. Retitled "The Keys of Kai" in 1966. Sold direct on second submission to *The Saint Magazine* in 1966, for $85.00. Jacobi received payment on 10 February 1967.

"The Player at Yellow Silence," *Galaxy Magazine* (Vol. 30, No. 3, June, 1970), pp. 4-14 , 150-152.
Science fantasy. 4,000 words. Longer version sent to agent Scott Meredith in 1966. Rewritten and shortened from 5,000 to 4,000 words in 1967. Tried direct at *Amazing Stories* in 1968. Sold by agent Virginia Kidd for $159.00, of which Jacobi received $143.10.

"The Cocomacaque," *The Arkham Collector,* ed. August Derleth (No. 8, Winter, 1971), pp. 223-232.
Weird. 3,000 words. Sold direct first trip out for $50.00. Saddle-stitched magazine published by Arkham House.

"The Music Lover," *Weird Tales* (Vol. 47, No. 4, Summer, 1974), pp. 2-8.
Weird. 3,500 words. Tried at *Playboy* in 1968. Sold by agent Virginia Kidd in 1973, for $70.00, of which Jacobi received $63.00.

"McIver's Fancy," *Mike Shayne Mystery Magazine* (Vol. 39, No. 6, December, 1976), pp. 83-90.
Mystery. 3,000 words. Original title: "The Chadwick Pit." Longer weird version revised as a straight mystery yarn, shortened from 4,500 to 3,000 words, and retitled "McIver's Fancy." Sold first trip out by agent Kirby McCauley for $45.00, of which Jacobi received $40.50. The original weird version was eventually published as "The Pit" in Lin Carter's paperback anthology, *Weird Tales #1* (1980).

"The Riburi Hat," *Mike Shayne Mystery Magazine* (Vol. 48, No. 1, January, 1984), pp. 52-68.
Detective. 6,500 words. Written in 1981. Tried by agent Kirby McCauley at *Ellery Queen's Mystery Magazine* in 1983. Sold by McCauley on 6 October 1983, for $100.00, payable upon acceptance, of which Jacobi received $90.00.

"The Lavalier," *Mike Shayne Mystery Magazine* (Vol. 48, No. 3, March, 1984), pp. 83-90.
Detective. 3,000 words. Featuring Jo Domingo of the Trinidad Constabulary, the protagonist of "The Legation Cigar" (*The Saint Detective Magazine,* August, 1957). Tried by agent Kirby McCauley at *Ellery Queen's Mystery Magazine* in 1983. Sold by McCauley on 6 October 1983, for $50.00, payable upon acceptance, of which Jacobi received $45.00.

Jacobi's files indicate that two additional stories were sold to newspapers. The author has been unable to verify whether or not they were ever published.

"Man Hasn't Changed"
Domestic. 2,000-word short-short. Original title: "Forever Man." Tried at *Liberty* (rejection slip), *Illustrated Love* (rejection slip), and *Abbott's Monthly* (rejection slip)

in 1933. Retitled "Man Hasn't Changed." Sold by agent Otis Adelbert Kline to United Features Syndicate on 15 January 1936, for $10.00, of which Jacobi received $8.50 on 27 January 1936.

"The Personality of Miss Prentiss"
Romance. 5,000 words. Alternate title: "The Personality of Miss Prudence." In a letter dated 2 April 1953, Jacobi told August Derleth that the *New Zealand Woman's Weekly* had purchased the story. This newspaper has informed the author (in a letter dated 11 February 1983) that the story was apparently never used.

III. *Fan Magazine Publications*

A. *Fiction*

"The Man from Makassar," *Marvel Tales*, ed. William L. Crawford (Vol. 1, No. 5, Summer, 1935), pp. 251-257.
Weird. 5,400 words. Working title: "The Unholy Operation." Tried at *Strange Tales* (got past editor Harry Bates but not publisher William Clayton), *Weird Tales* (leters dated 21 September 1931, 9 January and 18 October 1932, and 26 January 1933), *Dime Mystery Magazine* (rejection slip), and *Astounding Stories* (rejection slip). Contributed to *Unusual Stories* without charge. Published in *Unusual Stories'* companion magazine, *Marvel Tales*.

"Eternity When?," *WT50: A Tribute to Weird Tales,* ed. Robert Weinberg (1974), pp. 115-116.
Weird. 1,500-word short-short. Written in 1948. Tried at *Collier's* (brief letter), *This Week* (rejection slip), *The American* (brief letter), *The Blue Book Magazine* and *Best Years* (letter dated 10 April 1949). Contributed to *WT50* without charge, but received token payment of $5.00.

"Hamadryad," *Whispers,* ed. Dr. Stuart Schiff (Vol. 2, Nos. 2-3, June, 1975), pp. 27-36.
Weird. 4,000 words. Sold direct first trip out for $40.00.

"Test Case," *Midnight Sun,* ed. Gary Hoppenstand (Vol. 1, No. 2, Summer-Fall, 1975), pp. 89-96.
Science fiction. 4,000 words. Sold direct first trip out for $200.00.

"The Aquarium," *Fantasy Crossroads #7,* ed. Jonathan Bacon (February, 1976), pp. 18-22.
Weird. 3,500 words. Sold direct first trip out for $50.00. Unedited Cthulhu version of a story which was first published in August Derleth's anthology, *Dark Mind, Dark Heart* (1962), and was reprinted in Jacobi's collection, *Disclosures in Scarlet* (1972).

"Canal," *Starwind Magazine,* ed. Warren DiLeo (Vol. 1, No. 2, Spring, 1976), pp. 20-25.
Science fantasy. 5,500 words. First published in *Startling Stories* (Spring, 1944). Sold for reprint for $25.00.

"Satan's Roadhouse," *Weird Menace Classics #2,* ed. Robert Weinberg (1977), pp. 6-28.
Horror detective. 13,000-word novelette. First published in *Terror Tales* (October, 1934). Sold for reprint for $50.00.

"Forsaken Voyage," *Midnight Sun Five,* ed. Gary Hoppenstand (1979), pp. 29-35.

Sea adventure. 3,300 words. Original title: "Forsaken Cruise." Written in 1941. Longer version tried by agent Lurton Blassingame at *Maclean's Magazine* in 1941. Blassingame returned the manuscript after trying all available markets. Tried at *Argosy* (letter from editor Rogers Terrill in 1943). Revised, shortened from 5,000 to 4,500 words and retitled "Glory Passage" in 1946. Tried at *Argosy, Doc Savage,* and *Short Stories* in 1946. Tried at *Short Stories* in 1947. Sold direct to *Peace Force* (a magazine published on behalf of the United Nations) in 1950, but the manuscript was returned when the magazine ceased publication. Revised and retitled "The Last Cruise of the Trinidad Castle" in 1956. Tried at *Short Stories Magazine* (letter from editor Cylvia Kleinman in 1958, indicating that the magazine was doing poorly). Shortened from 4,500 to 3,300 words and retitled "Forsaken Voyage" in 1978. Sold direct for $165.00.

"The Syndicate of the Snake," *Etchings and Odysseys: A Special Tribute to Weird Tales,* ed. Eric A. Carlson, John J. Koblas, and R. Alain Everts (1983), pp. 8-15.
    Terror detective. 6,000 words. Original title: "Syndicate of the Snake." Written in 1937. Aimed at *Strange Detective Mysteries.* Sent to agent Lurton Blassingame on 30 September 1937. Contributed to *Etchings and Odysseys* in 1983 without charge.

"The Phantom from 512," *Shudder Stories,* ed. Robert M. Price (No. 1, June, 1984), pp. 33-40.
    Terror. 4,500 words. Aimed at *Thrilling Mystery.* Tried by agent Lurton Blassingame at *Thrilling Mystery* (letter from editor Leo Margulies in 1939). Sold direct to Robert M. Price on 28 March 1984, for $50.00, payable upon acceptance.

B. *Non-Fiction*

"The Science-Weird Controversy," *The Fantasite,* ed. Phil Bronson (Vol. 1, No. 3, April, 1941), pp. 7-8.
    In this publication of the Minneapolis Fantasy Society, Jacobi examines the rivalry between science-fiction and weird fans—a conflict which finds little support among the writers, since the term "fantasy" is used as a general classification for both types of fiction. Discusses H. P. Lovecraft, August Derleth, and Donald Wandrei.

"A Proposal," *The Fantasite,* ed. Phil Bronson (Vol. 2, No. 1, March-April, 1942), pp. 15-16, 20.
    In this publication of the Minneapolis Fantasy Society, Jacobi advocates the compilation of a science-fiction handbook as a means of standardizing terminology and topography.

"Memories of August," *IS six,* ed. Tom Collins (1972), pp. 26-29.
    Autobiographical, with emphasis on August Derleth.

"Rambling Memoirs," *The Diversifier,* ed. C. C. Clingan (Vol. III, No. 5, July, 1977), pp. 30-33.
    Autobiographical.

"The Derleth Connection," *The August Derleth Society Newsletter,* ed. Richard H. Fawcett (Vol. 4, No. 4, June, 1981), pp. 4-6.
    Autobiographical, with emphasis on August Derleth.

"Some Correspondence," *Etchings and Odysseys: A Special Tribute to Weird Tales,* ed. Eric A. Carlson, John J. Koblas, and R. Alain Everts (1983), pp. 96-97. Autobiographical.

IV. *Book Publications*

Stories in anthologies and collections are reprints unless otherwise indicated. All are hard cover unless otherwise noted.

A. *Anthologies*

Cook, Luella B. *Experiments in Writing: A High-School Textbook in Composition for the Junior and Senior Years.* New York and Chicago: Harcourt, Brace and Company, 1927.
   Although not strictly speaking an anthology, this textbook reprints Jacobi's first three stories from Central High School's *The Quest:* "The Runaway Box Car" (pp. 177-180), "The Lost Tapestry" (pp. 198-202), and "The Derelict" (pp. 214-216). Written and compiled by one of his former teachers, and published during his freshman year at the University of Minnesota.

Derleth, August, ed. *Sleep No More: Twenty Masterpieces of Horror for the Connoisseur.* "The Cane." New York: Farrar & Rinehart, Inc., 1944, pp. 227-243.
   First published in *Weird Tales* (April, 1934). Sold for reprint for $10.00. Omitted from the British paperback of the same title published by Panther Books in 1964; and from *Stories From Sleep No More,* a paperback published by Bantam Books in 1967.

Derleth, August, ed. *Sleep No More.* "The Cane." New York: Armed Services Edition, 1944, pp. 241-256. Paperback.
   Sold for reprint for $10.00. Jacobi received payment in June, 1945.

Derleth, August, ed. *The Sleeping & the Dead: Thirty Uncanny Tales.* "Carnaby's Fish." Chicago: Pellegrini & Cudahy, 1947, pp. 151-163.
   First published in *Weird Tales* (July, 1945). Sold for reprint in November, 1946, for $25.00, of which Jacobi and August Derleth each received $12.50.

Derleth, August, ed. *Strange Ports of Call.* "The Lost Street." New York: Pellegrini & Cudahy, 1948, pp. 276-290.
   Collaboration between Clifford D. Simak and Jacobi. First published as "The Street That Wasn't There" in *Comet* (July, 1941). Sold for reprint for $30.00, of which each author received $15.00 in 1947. Omitted from the paperback of the same title published by Berkley Books in 1958.

Cerf, Bennett, ed. *The Unexpected.* "Revelations in Black." New York: Bantam Books, 1948, pp. 230-254. Paperback.
   First published in *Weird Tales* (April, 1933). Sold for reprint for $35.00, of which Jacobi and August Derleth each received $17.50. Jacobi was in good company with O. Henry, Ambrose Bierce, Lord Dunsany, Dorothy L. Sayers, Robert Bloch, A. E. Coppard, and others. As of 11 January 1952, the book had sold 285,578 copies.

Derleth, August, ed. *Far Boundaries: 20 Science-Fiction Stories.* "Tepondicon." New York: Pellegrini & Cudahy, 1951, pp. 131-147.
   First published in *Planet Stories* (Winter Issue, September-November, 1946). Sold for reprint for $25.00.

Derleth, August, ed. *Far Boundaries.* "Tepondicon." Toronto: George J. McLeod, Ltd., 1951, pp. not known.

Derleth, August, ed. *Night's Yawning Peal: A Ghostly Company.* "The La Prello Paper." Sauk City, Wisconsin: Arkham House Publishers, 1952, pp. 46-56.
First published in *Weird Tales* (March, 1948). Sold for reprint for $25.00. Arkham House book published in conjunction with Pellegrini & Cudahy.

Derleth, August, ed. *Worlds of Tomorrow: Science-Fiction with a Difference.* "The Gentleman Is an Epwa." New York: Pellegrini & Cudahy, 1953, pp. 145-165.
Science fiction. 5,500 words. Revised according to August Derleth's suggestions. Sold direct first trip out for $35.00, of which Jacobi received $31.50 and agent Scott Meredith, who had made corrections, received $3.50. First appearance. Later reprinted in *Cosmos Science Fiction and Fantasy* (November, 1953). Omitted from the hardbound British reprint, *Worlds of Tomorrow,* published by Weidenfeld & Nicolson in 1954.

Derleth, August, ed. *Time To Come: Science-Fiction Stories of Tomorrow.* "The White Pinnacle." New York: Farrar, Straus and Young, 1954, pp. 207-231.
Science fiction. 6,000 words. Sold first trip out by agent Scott Meredith for $50.00, of which Jacobi received $45.00. Received an additional $6.52 in 1965. First appearance.

Derleth, August, ed. *Worlds of Tomorrow.* "The Gentleman Is an Epwa." New York: Berkley Publishing Corp., 1958, pp. 78-96. Paperback.
Sold for reprint for $25.00, of which Jacobi received $22.50 and August Derleth received $2.50.

Derleth, August, ed. *Time To Come.* "The White Pinnacle." New York: Berkley Publishing Corp., 1958, pp. 137-153. Paperback.
Omitted from the paperback of the same title published by Tower Books in 1965.

Charteris, Leslie, ed. *The Saint Mystery Library.* "The Legation Cigar." New York: Great American Publications, Inc., 1959, pp. 126-138. Paperback.
First published in *The Saint Detective Magazine* (August, 1957). Sold for reprint by agent Scott Meredith for $40.00, of which Jacobi received $36.00 (as much as the original sale). As No. 118 marked the first appearance of this series, this edition is identified as both No. 122 and No. 5. The title of its featured story, Baynard Kendrick's "Murder Made in Moscow," dominates both spine and front cover.

Derleth, August, ed. *Dark Mind, Dark Heart.* "The Aquarium." Sauk City, Wisconsin: Arkham House Publishers, 1962, pp. 134-147.
Weird. 3,500 words. Sold direct first trip out for $50.00 First appearance. Reference to Cthulhu deleted by August Derleth. Unedited version later published in *Fantasy Crossroads* #7 (February, 1976).

Derleth, August, ed. *When Evil Wakes: A New Anthology of the Macabre.* "The Kite." London: Souvenir Press, 1963, pp. 134-143.
First published as "Satan's Kite" in *Thrilling Mystery* (June, 1937).

Derleth, August, ed. *When Evil Wakes.* "The Kite." Toronto: Ryerson Press, 1963, pp. not known.

Cerf, Bennett, ed. *Stories Selected From The Unexpected.* "Revelations in

Black." New York: Bantam Books, 1963, pp. not known. Paperback.
Reprint of seventeen stories from *The Unexpected* (1948).

Derleth, August, ed. *New Worlds For Old*. "The Gentleman Is an Epwa." Four Square Books. London: The New English Library Limited, 1963, pp. 23-37. Paperback.
Sold for reprint for $10.00. Reprint of nine stories from *Worlds of Tomorrow* (1953).

Derleth, August, ed. *Dark Mind Dark Heart*. "The Aquarium." London: Mayflower Books Ltd., 1963, pp. 123-134. Paperback.
Sold for reprint for $16.00. Reissued in 1966.

Derleth, August, ed. *Over the Edge*. "Kincaid's Car." Sauk City, Wisconsin: Arkham House Publishers, 1964, pp. 142-160.
Science fiction. 5,000 words. Written 1957-1959. Revised according to August Derleth's suggestions in 1960. Sent to agent Scott Meredith in April, 1960. Sold direct first trip out on 6 July 1963, for $50.00. First appearance.

Derleth, August, ed. *The Unquiet Grave*. "Carnaby's Fish." Four Square Books. London: The New English Library Limited, 1964, pp. 31-43. Paperback.
Sold for reprint for $8.00. Reprint of fifteen stories from *The Sleeping & the Dead* (1947).

Protter, Eric, ed. *Monster Festival*. "Revelations in Black." New York: Vanguard Press, 1965, pp. 67-93.
Sold for reprint for $22.50.

Derleth, August, ed. *Far Boundaries*. "Tepondicon." Consul Books. London: World Distributors, 1965, pp. 109-121. Paperback.
Sold for reprint for $13.00.

Derleth, August, ed. *Night's Yawning Peal*. "The La Prello Paper." Consul Books. London: World Distributors, 1965, pp. 51-61. Paperback.

Derleth, August, ed. *When Evil Wakes: A New Anthology of the Macabre*. "The Kite." Corgi Books. London: Transworld Publishers Ltd, 1965, pp. 104-111. Paperback.
Sold for reprint for $15.00. Reissued in 1971 and 1977.

Barter, Alan F. and Raymond Wilson, eds. *Untravelled Worlds: An Anthology of Science Fiction*. "The Gentleman Is an Epwa." New York: St. Martin's Press, 1966, pp. 94-110. Paperback.
Sold for reprint. The amount Jacobi received is not known. Reissued in 1971.

Derleth, August, ed. *Travellers By Night*. "The Unpleasantness at Carver House." Sauk City, Wisconsin: Arkham House Publishers, 1967, pp. 120-137.
Weird. 5,000 words. Sold direct first trip out on 1 June 1965, for $50.00. First appearance.

Collins, Charles M., ed. *A Feast of Blood*. "Revelations in Black." New York: Avon Books, 1967, pp. 115-134. Paperback.
Sold for reprint for $30.00. Reissued (no date given) with new pagination ("Revelations in Black" on pp. 108-126).

$\mathcal{P}$ortrait in Moonlight

BY CARL JACOBI

THE Trinidad offices of Holworth and Company, Importers and Exporters, in Weightson Road near the Port-of-Spain waterfront, were under the capable, if unprogressive, managership of Rupert Clarkson. Clarkson, in his forty-sixth year, was a widower and a rather moody individual, with a tall, loose-jointed frame, narrow shoulders, and lonely eyes. He lived in Queen's Park West, quite a distance from the Holworth offices, but he always chose to walk, claiming that he needed the exercise.

As a matter of fact, there were a number of things Clarkson felt he needed. He was in a word growing old, and none realized it more than he. There were lines and crow's feet about his eyes. He had developed a slight stoop, probably from bending for long hours over a desk, and his hair was graying rapidly.

Psychologically, Clarkson knew that he should accept these changes as a matter of course, but somehow he couldn't do that. He was still young in spirit, and the knowledge that his material body was showing some signs of wear, however slight, greatly concerned him. The bureau in his bedroom was littered with bottles of restorers, dyes, and other masculine cosmetics, all of which he had given a trial and then discarded as either worthless or too obvious in their effect.

"It's this infernal sticky heat," he said on more than one occasion. "It ages one. Trinidad is no place for a white man."

Fearful of getting into a rut, Clarkson varied the course of his walk to work each day. But he always stopped at the corner of Dundonald Street and Tragarete Road to watch an aged Negro man stand before an

So many things don't make sense here on the islands; or make a frightful sense beyond mortal detection.

66

Heading by LEE BROWN COYE

Weird Tales (November, 1947)

Derleth, August, ed. *Far Boundaries.* "Tepondicon." London: Sphere Books, 1967, pp. 95-107. Paperback.

Derleth, August, ed. *Over the Edge.* "Kincaid's Car." London: Victor Gollancz Ltd, 1967, pp. 142-160.
Sold for reprint for $15.00. Received an additional $10.00 in 1968.

Derleth, August, ed. *Travellers By Night.* "The Unpleasantness at Carver House." London: Victor Gollancz Ltd, 1968, pp. 120-137.
Sold for reprint for $10.00.

Derleth, August, ed. *Time To Come: Science-Fiction Stories of Tomorrow.* "The White Pinnacle." New York: Pyramid Books, 1969, pp. 145-163. Paperback.

Derleth, August, ed. *Dark Things.* "The Singleton Barrier." Sauk City, Wisconsin: Arkham House Publishers, 1971, pp. 131-144.
Weird. 5,000 words. Sold direct first trip out on 8 November 1967, for $50.00. First appearance.

Dickie, James, ed. *The Undead.* "Revelations in Black." London: Neville Spearman, 1971, pp. not known.
Sold for reprint. The amount Jacobi received is not known.

Olney, Ross R., ed. *Ten Tales Calculated to Give You Shudders.* "The Last Drive." A Whitman Book. Racine, Wisconsin: Western Publishing Company, Inc., 1972, pp. 132-140.
First published in *Weird Tales* (June, 1933). Sold for reprint in 1969, for $25.00.

Dickie, James, ed. *The Undead.* "Revelations in Black." London: Pan Books, 1973, pp. 106-130. Paperback.
Sold for reprint. The amount Jacobi received is not known.

Page, Gerald W., ed. *Nameless Places.* "Chameleon Town." Sauk City, Wisconsin: Arkham House, 1975, pp. 214-227.
Weird. 5,500 words. Sold direct first trip out for $50.00. First appearance.

Carr, Terry, ed. *Creatures from Beyond: Nine Stories of Science Fiction and Fantasy.* "The Street That Wasn't There." Nashville and New York: Thomas Nelson Inc., Publishers, 1975, pp. 117-135.
Sold for reprint. The amount Jacobi received is not known.

McCauley, Kirby, ed. *Night Chills: Stories of Suspense and Horror.* "The Face in the Wind." New York: Avon Books, 1975, pp. 169-191. Paperback.
First published in *Weird Tales* (April, 1936). Sold for reprint. The amount Jacobi received is not known.

Dickie, James, ed. *The Undead.* "Revelations in Black." New York: Pocket Books, 1976, pp. 105-129.
Sold for reprint. The amount Jacobi received is not known.

Parry, Michel, ed. *Spaced Out.* "Smoke of the Snake." Panther Books. St Albans: Granada Publishing Limited, 1977, pp. 105-124. Paperback.
First published in *Top-Notch* (January, 1934). Sold for British reprint by agent Kirby McCauley for $115.00, of which Jacobi received $103.00 on 4 April 1983.

Derleth, August, ed. *When Evil Wakes: A New Anthology of the Macabre.* "The Kite." London: Sphere Books, 1977, pp. 119-128. Paperback.

Matheson, Richard and Jack C. Haldeman II, eds. *Rod Serling's Other Worlds.* "The Royal Opera House." New York: Bantam Books, Inc., 1978, pp. 61-73. Paperback. (Introduction by Richard Matheson, story notes by Jack C. Haldeman II.) First published in Jacobi's collection, *Disclosures in Scarlet* (1972). Sold for reprint by agent Kirby McCauley. The amount Jacobi received is not known.

Schiff, Stuart, ed. *Whispers II.* "The Elcar Special." Garden City, New York: Doubleday & Company, Inc., 1979, pp. 125-131. Weird. 3,500 words. Sold direct first trip out to publisher Stan Lee of the Marvel Comics Group for *The Haunt of Horror* in 1974, payable upon publication, but remained unpublished when the magazine adopted a comic book format and began phasing out fiction. Sold direct to Stuart Schiff. The amount Jacobi received is not known. First appearance.

Pronzini, Bill, ed. *Voodoo! A Chrestomathy of Necromancy.* "The Digging at Pistol Key." New York: Arbor House, 1980, pp. 82-100. First published in *Weird Tales* (July, 1947). Sold for reprint. The amount Jacobi received is not known.

Carter, Lin, ed. *Weird Tales #1.* "The Pit." Zebra Books. New York: Kensington Publishing Corp., 1980, pp. 130-148. Paperback. Weird. 4,500 words. Original title: "The Chadwick Pit." Sold first trip out by agent Kirby McCauley for $135.00, of which Jacobi received $121.50. First appearance. A shorter version (without the weird angle) had been published as "McIver's Fancy" in *Mike Shayne Mystery Magazine* (December, 1976). Continuity between the original *Weird Tales*, the four-issue revival of 1973-1974, and this four-issue paperback series is maintained through volume and numbering system (this "issue" appeared as Vol. 48, No. 1, Spring, 1981).

Pronzini, Bill, ed. *The Arbor House Necropolis.* "The Digging at Pistol Key." New York: Arbor House, 1981, pp. 101-117. Sold for reprint. The amount Jacobi received is not known.

Carter, Lin, ed. *Weird Tales # 3.* "The Black Garden." Zebra Books. New York: Kensington Publishing Corp., 1981, pp. 139-163. Paperback. Weird. 5,500 words. Working title: "The Woman in Black." Sold first trip out by agent Kirby McCauley for $165.00, of which Jacobi received $148.50. First appearance. Continuity between the original *Weird Tales,* the four-issue revival of 1973-1974, and this four-issue paperback series is maintained through volume and numbering system (this "issue" appeared as Vol. 48, No. 3, Fall, 1981).

B. *Collections*

Jacobi, Carl. *Revelations in Black.* Sauk City, Wisconsin: Arkham House, 1947, 272 pp., $3.00. Jacket illustration by Ronald Clyne.
"Revelations in Black." First published in *Weird Tales* (April, 1933).
"Phantom Brass." First published in *Railroad Stories* (August, 1934).
"The Cane." First published in *Weird Tales* (April, 1934).
"The Coach on the Ring." First published as "The Haunted Ring" in *Ghost Stories* (December, 1931-January, 1932). Original title restored by Jacobi.
"The Kite." First published as "Satan's Kite" in *Thrilling Mystery* (June, 1937). Original title restored by Jacobi.

"Canal." First published in *Startling Stories* (Spring, 1944).

"The Satanic Piano." First published in *Weird Tales* (May, 1934).

"The Last Drive." First published in *Weird Tales* (June, 1933).

"The Spectral Pistol." First published as "The Phantom Pistol" in *Weird Tales* (May, 1941). Jacobi substituted this title for the original in a letter to August Derleth dated 7 September 1945.

"Sagasta's Last." First published in *Strange Stories* (August, 1939).

"The Tomb from Beyond." First published in *Wonder Stories* (November, 1933).

"The Digging at Pistol Key." First published in *Weird Tales* (July, 1947).

"Moss Island." First published in *The Quest* (May, 1930) and *Amazing Stories Quarterly* (Winter, 1932).

"Carnaby's Fish." First published in *Weird Tales* (July, 1945).

"The King and the Knave." First published as "The Devil Deals" in *Weird Tales* (April, 1938). Original title restored by Jacobi.

"Cosmic Teletype." First published in *Thrilling Wonder Stories* (October, 1938).

"A Pair of Swords." First published in *Weird Tales* (August, 1933).

"A Study in Darkness." First published as "Spawn of Blackness" in *Strange Stories* (October, 1939). Jacobi substituted this title for the original in a letter to August Derleth dated 6 August 1945.

"Mive." First published in *Minnesota Quarterly* (Fall, 1928) and *Weird Tales* (January, 1932).

"Writing on the Wall." First published as "The Cosmic Doodler" in *Startling Stories* (Fall, 1944). Jacobi substituted this title for the original, after he considered retitling it "The Space Doodler," in a letter to August Derleth dated 7 September 1945.

"The Face in the Wind." First published in *Weird Tales* (April, 1936).

Jacobi, Carl. *Portraits in Moonlight.* Sauk City, Wisconsin: Arkham House, 1964, 213 pp. $4.00. Jacket illustration by Frank Utpatel.

"Portrait in Moonlight." First published in *Weird Tales* (November, 1947).

"Witches in the Cornfield." First published as "The Dangerous Scarecrow" in *Imagination* (August, 1954). Original title restored by Jacobi.

"The Martian Calendar." First published in *Space Science Fiction Magazine* (Spring, 1957).

"The Corbie Door." First published in *Weird Tales* (May, 1947).

"Tepondicon." First published in *Planet Stories* (Winter Issue, September-November, 1946).

"Incident at the Galloping Horse." First published in *Weird Tales* (November, 1948).

"Made in Tanganyika." First published in *Fantastic Universe* (May, 1954).

"Matthew South and Company." First published in *Weird Tales* (May, 1949).

"Long Voyage." First published as "The Long Voyage" in *Fantastic Universe* (September, 1955). Original title restored by Jacobi.

"The Historian." First published in *Startling Stories* (May, 1950).

"Lodana." First published in *Startling Stories* (September, 1947).

"The Lorenzo Watch." First published in *Weird Tales* (January, 1948).

"The La Prello Paper." First published in *Weird Tales* (March, 1948).

"The Spanish Camera." First published in *Weird Tales* (September, 1950).

Jacobi, Carl. *Disclosures in Scarlet.* Sauk City, Wisconsin: Arkham House, 1972, 181 pp., $5.00. Jacket illustration by Frank Utpatel.

"The Aquarium." First published in August Derleth's anthology, *Dark Mind, Dark Heart* (1962).

"The Player at Yellow Silence." First published in *Galaxy Magazine* (June, 1970).

"The Unpleasantness at Carver House." First published in August Derleth's anthology, *Travellers By Night* (1967).

"The Cocomacaque." First published in *The Arkham Collector* (Winter, 1971).

"The Gentleman Is an Epwa." First published in August Derleth's anthology, *Worlds of Tomorrow* (1953).

"The Royal Opera House." Science fantasy. 3,500 words. Working title: "The Troy-Celeste Experiment." Written 1963-1965. Tried at *Amazing Stories* in 1966. First appearance.

"Strangers to Straba." First published in *Fantastic Universe* (October, 1954).

"Exit Mr. Smith." First published as "He Looked Back" in *If* (August, 1966). Original title restored by Jacobi.

"Gentlemen, the Scavengers." First published as "Gentlemen, the Scavengers!" in *Thrilling Wonder Stories* (April, 1948).

"Round Robin." Science fantasy. 2,800 words. Working title: "The Satellite Writers." Written in 1966. First appearance.

"The White Pinnacle." First published in August Derleth's anthology, *Time To Come* (1954).

"Mr. Iper of Hamilton." Science fantasy. 2,700 words. Working title: "The Dancing Dolls." Written in 1966. First appearance.

"The War of the Weeds." First published in *Thrilling Wonder Stories* (February, 1939).

"Kincaid's Car." First published in August Derleth's anthology, *Over the Edge* (1964).

"The Random Quantity." First published in *Avon Fantasy Reader No. 5* (1947).

"Sequence." Science fiction. 2,500 words. Original title: "The Visitors." Tried at *Thrilling Wonder Stories* (letter from editor Sam Merwin, Jr., in 1950). Jacobi substituted this title for the original. First appearance.

"The Singleton Barrier." First published in August Derleth's anthology, *Dark Things* (1971).

Jacobi, Carl. *Revelations in Black.* Jersey: Neville Spearman, 1974, 272 pp. British reprint.

Jacobi, Carl. *Revelations in Black.* Panther Books. St Albans: Granada Publishing Limited, 1977, 141 pp. Paperback.
First volume of a two-volume British reprint.

Jacobi, Carl. *The Tomb from Beyond.* Panther Books. St Albans: Granada Publishing Limited, 1977, 144 pp. Paperback.
Second volume of a two-volume British reprint of *Revelations in Black.*

Jacobi, Carl. *Revelations in Black.* A Jove/HBJ Book. New York: Jove Publications, Inc., 1979, 317 pp. Paperback.

C. *Non-Fiction*

Jacobi, Carl, ed. *Paths to the Far East.* Minneapolis: Social Studies, Minneapolis Board of Education, 1940, 124 pp.
With interest in the Far East mounting in 1938, the Social Studies department of the Minneapolis Board of Education asked Jacobi to write, compile, and edit data and background material on the Orient. This 8½" x 11" soft cover textbook was used throughout the war years in Minneapolis junior high schools. Profusely illustrated with maps, charts, and pulp magazine drawings.

V. *Selected Foreign Publications*

A. *Magazines*

"Resa pa Narri," *Tidsfordrif* (No. 31, 18 August 1938), pp. 49-51.
Swedish translation of "Ticket to Nowhere." Sold for reprint by agent Otis
Adelbert Kline to this Goteborg magazine for $5.00, of which Jacobi received $4.00.

"Beatrice et la cartomancienne," *La Patrie,* 27 August 1949, pp. 1, 6, 8, 11
(magazine section).
French translation of "Her Impulse Day." Sold for reprint by *Star Weekly* to this
Montreal newspaper. The amount Jacobi received is not known.

B. *Anthologies*

Roth, Max, M. E. Coindreau, Alyette Guillot-Coli, and Rene Wintzen, eds.
Histoires insolites. "Le cerf-volant." Paris: Casterman, 1964, pp. 195-209.
French translation of "The Kite." Sold for reprint on 14 March 1964, for $15.00.

Papy, Jacques, ed. *Histoires d'outre-monde.* "Le Camee" and "Celaeno." Paris:
Casterman, 1966, pp. 93-104, 239-262.
French translations of "The Coach on the Ring" and "The Face in the Wind."
Sold for reprint on 16 May 1964, for $42.00.

Las mejores historias insolitas. "La Cometa." Barcelona: Editorial Brugera,
1966, pp. 505-516. Paperback. (Editor not listed.)
Spanish translation of "The Kite." Sold for reprint for $10.00 Reissued in 1967,
1969, 1970, 1972, 1973, and 1974.

Papy, Jacques, ed. *Nouvelles histoires d'outre-monde.* "La Porte des corbeaux,"
"Le Mausolee," "Meurtre dans le champ de mais," "Matthew South et Cie," and
"Ailes d'ebene." Paris: Casterman, 1967, pp. 17-42, 43-62, 161-169, 171-183, 231-237.
French translations of "The Corbie Door," "The Tomb from Beyond," "Witches
in the Cornfield," "Matthew South and Company," and "Mive." Sold for reprint for
$52.00.

Prins, Aart C., ed. *De bewoner van het meer en andere griezelverhalen.* "De
Theorie van La Prello." Utrecht and Antwerp: A. W. Bruna & Zoon, 1968, pp. 135-148.
Paperback.
Dutch translation of "The La Prello Paper." Sold for reprint. The amount Jacobi
received is not known.

Papy, Jacques, ed. *Vingt pas dans l'au-dela.* "La Canne," "Revelations en noir,"
"Le Pistolet fantome," and "Le Tresor du pirate." Paris: Casterman, 1970, pp. 74-88,
231-252, 253-267, 299-314.
French translations of "The Cane," "Revelations in Black," "The Phantom
Pistol," and "The Digging at Pistol Key." Sold for reprint for $44.00.

Jensen, Jorgen, ed. *10 saelsomme lystfiskerhistorier.* "Carnabys fisk."
Spektrums Pocketboger. Copenhagen: Forlaget Spektrum, 1970, pp. 122-135.
Paperback.
Danish translation of "Carnaby's Fish." Sold for reprint for $15.00.

Sadoul, Jacques, ed. *Les meilleurs recits de Planet Stories.* "Tepondicon." Paris:
Editions J'ai Lu, 1975, pp. 87-104. Paperback.
French translation of "Tepondicon." Sold for reprint by agent Scott Meredith.
The amount Jacobi received is not known.

C. Collections

Jacobi, Carl. *Les ecarlates: contes.* "Revelations en noir," "La Montre," "La Ville cameleon," "Le Cocomacaque," "Le Portrait au clair de lune," "L'Attareil photographique," "Ca qui se tassa a Carver House," "La Porte aux corbeaux," "L'Aquarium," and "Le Visage dans le Vent." Paris: Librairie des Champs-Elysees, 1980, 247 pp. Paperback.

French translations of "Revelations in Black," "The Lorenzo Watch," "Chameleon Town," "The Cocomacaque," "Portrait in Moonlight," "The Spanish Camera," "The Unpleasantness at Carver House," "The Corbie Door," "The Aquarium," and "The Face in the Wind." Sold for reprint on 26 October 1978, for $416.65.

Jacobi's files indicate that several additional stories were sold abroad: "Phantom Brass" (sold for reprint to Denmark on 15 October 1948, for $12.00); "Revelations in Black" (sold for reprint to Sweden in 1963, for $10.00); "Redemption Trail" (in a letter to August Derleth dated 26 November 1963, Jacobi reported that this tale had appeared in Spanish translation, sold for reprint by agent Lurton Blassingame); "The Kite" (sold for reprint to Sweden on 30 November 1963, for $10.00); "The Kite" (sold for reprint to Norway on 15 February 1964, for $16.00); "The Aquarium" (sold for reprint to Italy in January, 1965); "The Kite" (sold for reprint to Finland in 1966, for $10.00); "The King and the Knave" (sold for reprint to Finland in 1968, for $54.00); and "The Tomb from Beyond" (sold for reprint to the Netherlands on 10 July 1970, for $15.00). The author has been unable to ascertain where they were published.

VI. Miscellaneous Publications

A. Interviews

"Etchings & Odysseys Interview: Carl Jacobi," *Etchings and Odysseys: A Tribute to the Weird,* ed. Eric Carlson and John Koblas (1973), pp. 46-50.

B. Autobiographical Sketches

Thrilling Wonder Stories (Vol. XIII, No. 3, June, 1939), p. 87.
Three paragraphs of autobiography with accompanying photograph.

"Introducing the Author," *Imagination* (Vol. 5, No. 8, August, 1954), pp. 2, 76-77.
Seven paragraphs of autobiography with accompanying photograph, in conjunction with "The Dangerous Scarecrow."

Pugmire, W. H., ed. *Carl Jacobi: An Appreciation.* "Foreword." Pensacola, Florida: Stellar Z Productions, 1977, pp. 3-4.
Ten paragraphs of autobiography with two accompanying photographs.

C. Letters to Editors

Short Stories (Vol. CLXII, No. 2, January 25, 1938), pp. 172-173.
In conjunction with "Holt Sails the 'San Hing'," Jacobi wrote, in "The Story Tellers' Circle" correspondence department, a largely autobiographical, seven-paragraph sketch, highlighting his exchange of letters with the commanding officers

of military outposts at Long Nawang, Borneo, and Ambunti, New Guinea.

Thrilling Wonder Stories (Vol. XII, No. 2, October, 1938), pp. 117, 129.
In "The Story Behind the Story" correspondence department, Jacobi explains what inspired him to write "Cosmic Teletype."

Thrilling Adventures (Vol. XXXI, No. 3, November, 1939), pp. 102-103.
In conjunction with "The Twenty-One Crescents," Jacobi contributed a letter to "The Globe Trotter" correspondence department, chronicling the existence of a lost Macedonian civilization hidden deep in the mountains and valleys of Baluchistan. Shangri-La fiction laced with generous portions of historical research. Jacobi once later remarked to the author, with a burst of laughter, "I wonder where the hell I got all that stuff!"

Thrilling Adventures (Vol. XLVI, No. 1, November, 1943), pp. 94-95.
In conjunction with "Black Lace," Jacobi contributed another letter to "The Globe Trotter," tracing the history of seventeenth-century Caribbean freebooters, including L'Ollinais, Edward Teach ("Blackbeard"), Bartholomew Roberts, Farrington Spriggs, and Henry Morgan.

Weird Tales (Vol. 47, No. 2, Fall, 1973), p. 94.
Brief letter to "The Eyrie" correspondence department, congratulating the magazine on its return to the stands in a pulp format.

D. *Humorous Sketches, Anecdotes, and Poems (All Published in the University of Minnesota's Humor Magazine, Ski-U-Mah)*

Ski-U-Mah frequently did not use by-lines, so that it would be impossible to identify Jacobi pieces if he had not circled his contributions in the copies he has preserved in his own files.

Vol. VII, No. 8, October, 1927 (misnumbered; should be No. 2)
Poem: "Old Faithful" (p. 15)

Vol. VII, No. 5, February, 1928
Sketch: "When You Call Me That, Smile" (p. 19)
Sketch: "Otto Supply Co." (p. 19)
Sketch: "At the Salesroom" (p. 22)
Two untitled anecdotes and untitled poem (p. 22)
Untitled anecdote (p. 27)
Sketch: "Hiram Buys a Car" (p. 32)
Sketch: "Evening of the Formal" (p. 32)
Sketch: "In Case Your Car Stops" (p. 32)

Vol. VII, No. 6, March, 1928
Untitled anecdote and untitled poem (p. 11)
Sketch: "A Coed's Dream" (p. 13)
Anecdote: "Use of the Comma" (p. 17)
Untitled anecdote (p. 17)
Sketch: "No Man's Land" (p. 19)
Anecdote: " 'Let's Hope Not' " (p. 21)

Vol. VII, No. 7, April, 1928
Filler: "Latest Books" (p. 7)
Untitled filler (p. 7)

Untitled filler (p. 15)
Sketch: "Psychology Lecture Notes" (p. 18)

Vol. VII, No. 8, May 10, 1928
Sketch: "Six Minutes Past Three" (p. 14)
Sketch: "Salesmanship" (p. 19)

Vol. VII, No. 9, June, 1928
Sketch: "Trot!" (p. 13)
Sketch: "American Mercury Stuff" (p. 33)

Vol. 8, No. 1, September, 1928
Sketch: "Ostracized" (p. 13)
Sketch: "Episode of the Match" (p. 38)

Vol. IX, No. 8, May, 1930
Two untitled anecdotes (p. 13)
Poem: "Modernized Shakespeare" (p. 20)
Sketch: "When You Call Me That, Smile—" (p. 24)
    Reprint. First published in February, 1928, issue.
Poem: "The Cravin' " (p. 28)
    Burlesque of Edgar Allan Poe.

E. *Book Reviews*

Ski-U-Mah (Vol. 8, No. 1, September, 1928), p. 35.
Favorable review of Carl Van Vetchen's *Spider Boy.*

Ski-U-Mah (Vol. 8, No. 3, November, 1928), p. 35.
Favorable review of A. E. W. Mason's *The Prisoner in the Opal.*

Ski-U-Mah (Vol. 8, No. 4, December, 1928), p. 34.
Favorable review of Augustus Muir's *The Shadow on the Left.*

Ski-U-Mah (Vol. 8, No. 5, January, 1929), p. 36.
Favorable reviews of Jeffery Farnol's *Guyfford of Weare* and O. E. Rolvaag's
Peter Victorious.

Ski-U-Mah (Vol. 8, No. 6, February, 1929), p. 27.
Strong praise for Arthur Machen's *The Hill of Dreams.*

Ski-U-Mah (Vol. 8, No. 7, March, 1929), p. 30.
Enthusiastic review of Maurice Leblanc's *Arsene Lupin Intervenes* and
favorable review of William Beebe's *Beneath Tropic Seas.*

Ski-U-Mah (Vol. 8, No. 9, May, 1929), p. 33.
Favorable reviews of Anne Douglas Sedgwick's *Dark Hester* and Johannes von
Guenther's *Cagliostro.*

"Factual Fantasies," *The Arkham Sampler*, ed. August Derleth (Vol. 2, No. 1,
Winter, 1949), pp. 85-86.
Favorable review of Patrick Mahony's *Out of the Silence.*

"Sleuth Solar Pons...'his last bow'," *Minneapolis Tribune,* June 10, 1973, p. 8D.
Enthusiastic review of August Derleth's *The Chronicles of Solar Pons.*

F. *Articles Written as a Reporter on the Minneapolis Star (January-March, 1931)*

A sampling of the most interesting headlines. The *Star* did not use by-lines during this period, so that it would be impossible to identify Jacobi pieces if he had not kept a thick scrapbook containing all of his writing for the *Star*.

" 'U' Scientist Relates Desert Search for Pueblo Relics " (January 19, 1931)
"Third Dimension Pictures Called Probability Soon"
"Student Fireman Turns Frat Fire Into Comedy"
"Campus Sees Gang Guns Flash—Police Don't Care"
"Patron Charges Cab Driver Beat Him"
"First Wife Ill, Mate Admits Bigamy"
"Vandals Steal Old Bell With Czar's Insignia"
"Grand Duchess of Russia Refuses to Discuss Soviets"
"Yeggs Routed by Watchman"
"Oriental's Glass Eye Lure at Morgue Sale"
"Vampires? They Have Them in Australia, Says Visitor" (March 5, 1931)
"Couple Defy Death in Fire to Rescue Seven"
"Lincoln Debate Remembered by Realty Man Here"
"Queen of Pioneers, 102, Wants Birthday Dance" (March 5, 1931)
"Grocery Manager Smashes Bandit on Jaw to Foil Daylight Holdup"
"Professor Slips From Classroom to Marry Co-ed"
"Princess Der Ling, From Chinese Court, to Speak"
"School Child Badly Hurt; Hit By Truck"
"Bandits Get Safe But Can't Open It"
"Messiah Claim Is Renounced"

G. *Other Writings*

West, Joseph A. *Pork Chops and Gravy.* "Introduction." Madison, Wisconsin: The Strange Company, 1984, unpaginated.

VII. *Unpublished Works*

All manuscripts are extant unless otherwise indicated.

"Armies of the Night"
Adventure. 700 words. Handwritten first draft dated 12 May 1925; handwritten revised draft dated 25 October 1925. One copy bound by Jacobi on 29 May 1925, as *Adventure on the High Seas* by Carl R. Jacobi, 26 pp., containing "The Derelict" (published in the May, 1925, issue of *The Quest*), "Armies of the Night," and "Adrift on the Sargasso."

"Adrift on the Sargasso"
Adventure. 1,100 words. Written in 1925. One copy bound by Jacobi on 29 May 1925, as *Adventure on the High Seas* by Carl R. Jacobi, 26 pp., containing "The Derelict" (published in the May, 1925, issue of *The Quest*), "Armies of the Night," and "Adrift on the Sargasso."

"Triple Transaction"
Detective. 5,400 words. Longer version tried (with "The Inverted Seven") at *Real Detective Tales* (letter from editor Edwin Baird in 1928, with the comment, "Both came close"). Shortened from 7,000 to 5,400 words and retitled "Enter Stephen Benedict." Published in *Minnesota Quarterly* (Winter, 1930).

"The Inverted Seven"
Detective. Tried (with "Triple Transaction") at *Real Detective Tales* (letter from editor Edwin Baird in 1928, with the comment, "Both came close"). Non-extant.

"Black Hyena"
Baluchistan adventure. 16,500-word novelette. Alternate titles: "The Shadow of the Black Hyena" and "Guns of the Hyena." Tried at *Oriental Stories* (letter from editor Farnsworth Wright dated 24 February 1932).

"The Clumsy Galoot"
Western. 4,600 words. Alternate titles: "Clumsy Galoot," "Clumsy Holdup," "A Matter of Grace," and "Stumblin' Steve." Originally planned as a collaboration between Jacobi and Hugh B. Cave. Sent to August Derleth on 9 June 1932. Revised according to Cave's suggestions and retitled "Clumsy Holdup." Tried at *Western Story Magazine* (rejection slip twice), *All Western Magazine* (rejection slip), *Worker's Fiction Magazine, Cowboy Stories* (rejection slip, then short letter), *Wild West Stories and Complete Novel Magazine* (rejection slip), and *Pete Rice Magazine* (rejection slip). Sent to agent Otis Adelbert Kline on 15 January 1936. Shortened from 4,600 to 3,500 words and retitled "Painted Holdup" in 1941. Sent on 30 August 1941 to agent Lurton Blassingame, who returned the manuscript for revision.

"We Find the Dead"
Adventure. 1,800 words. Original title: "Scavengers of Poppy Fields." Longer version tried at *Collier's*. Shortened from 3,200 to 1,800 words and retitled "We Find the Dead." Tried at *Weird Tales* (letter from Farnsworth Wright dated 3 February 1933).

"The Monument"
Weird. 3,000 words. Tried at *Weird Tales* (letter from Farnsworth Wright dated 18 February 1933).

"Phantom Brass"
Railroad weird. 2,500 words. Three variant endings, written prior to the published version in *Railroad Stories* (August, 1934).

"Blood Over the Footlights"
Horror mystery. 10,000-word novelette. Tried at Popular Publications (long letter from editor Rogers Terrill of *Dime Mystery Magazine* and *Terror Tales* in November, 1934, with the comment, "Not enough terror"). Sent to agent Otis Adelbert Kline, who returned the manuscript on 17 May 1937, after trying all available markets.

"The Death Wire"
Adventure. 4,300 words. Longer version tried at *Thrilling Adventures* (short note), *Doc Savage* (short note), and *Adventure* (rejection slip) in 1935. Retitled "Formosan Wires." Tried at *Dime Adventure Magazine* (good letter). Shortened from 5,000 to 4,300 words and retitled "Charged Wires." Tried at *Thrilling Adventures* in 1939.

"Dangerous Glamour" (by "Stephen Benedict")
Confession. 4,500 words. Aimed at *True Confessions Magazine*. Tried at *True Confessions Magazine* (letter in 1935, calling it "trite"). Sent on 15 January 1936 to agent Otis Adelbert Kline, who returned the manuscript. Retitled "I Model My Soul." Sent on 6 May 1937 to agent Lurton Blassingame, who returned the manuscript.

"Coffin Crag"

Horror detective. 12,000-word novelette. Featuring Stephen Benedict, the protagonist of "Satan's Roadhouse" (*Terror Tales,* October, 1934). Tried at *Terror Tales* (nice letter from editor Rogers Terrill stating he had recently published yarns with similar plots).

"River Renegade" (by "Richard East")
Adventure. 5,000 words. Alternate title: "Pawns of the River King." Tried by agent Lurton Blassingame at *Spicy-Adventure Stories.*

"Wings for a Sultan"
Borneo adventure. 6,000 words. Sent to agent Otis Adelbert Kline.

"Monkey Fag"
Borneo adventure. 3,000 words. Tried by agent Lurton Blassingame at *Thrilling Adventures, Doc Savage, Top-Notch, Short Stories,* and *Argosy* in 1936. Blassingame returned the manuscript on 2 June 1937, after trying all available markets.

"Rails of the Yellow Skull"
Terror mystery. 9,000-word novelette. Tried by agent Lurton Blassingame at *Dime Mystery Magazine* and *Ace Mystery Magazine* in 1936. Blassingame returned the manuscript on 2 June 1937. Revised and retitled "Terror Express." Sent to Blassingame.

"Snow Trail"
Western. 5,000 words. Sent on 19 November 1936 to agent Lurton Blassingame, who returned the manuscript after trying all available markets. Non-extant.

"Prisoners of Vibration"
Science fiction. 6,000 words. Tried at *Thrilling Wonder Stories* (good letter from editor Leo Margulies) and *Astounding Stories* in 1936. Tried at *Amazing Stories* (rejection slip) in 1938.

"Prize for Belly-Boy"
Borneo adventure. 2,500 words. Title suggested by August Derleth. Tried at *Esquire* (letter in 1936, claiming they had been using similar native yarns). Sent to agent Otis Adelbert Kline, who returned the manuscript after trying all available markets. Tried at *Tidsfordrif* in Sweden and *Esquire.*

"Deputy at Lost Brand"
Western. 5,000 words. Sent to agent Lurton Blassingame on 28 September 1936. Later sent to agent Otis Adelbert Kline, who returned the manuscript for revision.

"Borrowed Horse"
Western. 4,500 words.

"The Case of the Stolen Car"
Mystery satire. 2,500 words. Tried at *Esquire* (letter in 1937, with the comment, "Not quite").

"Heads, You Lose"
Borneo adventure. 5,000 words. Tried by agent Lurton Blassingame at *Short Stories, Dime Adventure Magazine, Argosy, Top-Notch, Thrilling Adventures, All-Star Adventure Magazine,* and *Doc Savage* in 1936-1937. Blassingame returned the manuscript on 2 June 1937, after trying all available markets.

"Heliograph"
Borneo adventure. 5,500 words. Tried at *Dime Adventure Magazine* (rejection slip) in 1937. Tried by agent Lurton Blassingame at *Short Stories, Top-Notch, Thrilling Adventures, South Sea Stories, Complete Stories, Argosy, Doc Savage,* and *All-Star Adventure Magazine.* Blassingame returned the manuscript on 2 June 1937, after trying all available markets. Revised and retitled "Soldier of the Sun." Sent to agent Otis Adelbert Kline.

"Woman of the Witch-Flowers"
Weird terror. 4,000 words. Aimed at *Eerie Stories.* Sent to agent Otis Adelbert Kline on 13 June 1937. Sold direct to Robert M. Price on 26 April, 1984, for $50.00, payable upon acceptance. Scheduled to appear in *Shudder Stories* (No. 2).

"Storm Warning"
Honduras adventure. 4,300 words. Alternate titles: "The Cage of Death," "Caged Death Spots," "Caged Despots," and "Diamonds with Spots." Aimed at *Doc Savage* or *The Skipper.* Tried by agent Lurton Blassingame at *Doc Savage* (letter in 1937, indicating they had already published a similar yarn). Blassingame returned the manuscript on 12 December 1938, after trying all available markets.

"The Nipper and the Narcissus"
Detective. 8,000-word novelette. Sent in August, 1937, to agent Lurton Blassingame, who returned the manuscript for revision. Jacobi considered it "a rather loose-jointed detective yarn of middling worth that probably won't sell." It didn't.

"Black Lace"
Weird pirate adventure. 10,000-word novelette. Original weird version of a story eventually published as a straight pirate yarn in *Thrilling Adventures* (November, 1943).

"Your Witness, Tuan"
Borneo adventure. 5,800 words. Aimed at *Short Stories.* Tried by agent Lurton Blassingame at *Short Stories, Argosy,* and *Thrilling Adventures* in 1938. Blassingame returned the manuscript on 12 December 1938, after trying all available markets. Retitled "Barrister in the Bush." Tried at *Thrilling Adventures* and *Doc Savage.* Revised (switching the setting from Borneo to the Belgian Congo) and retitled "Your Witness, Bwana" in 1942. Tried at *Jungle Stories.*

"The Bugle and the Belle"
Romantic adventure. 3,200 words. Longer version sent to agent Lurton Blassingame, who returned the manuscript for revision, in 1938. Revised. Blassingame returned the manuscript on 12 December 1938, after trying all available markets. Shortened from 5,000 to 3,200 words. Blassingame returned the manuscript again, claiming it did not have the proper war slant. Revised (given a Canadian angle). Tried at *Maclean's Magazine.* Retitled "Bugle Spray." Tried at *This Week.*

"Crash"
Domestic. 1,500 words. Revised and shortened from 2,200 to 1,500 words. Tried at *Collier's* (letter in December, 1938, calling the plot "obvious, transparent, and unpleasant"), *Esquire* (letter stating all but the ending was good), and *Redbook* (rejection slip). Sent to agent Otis Adelbert Kline, who returned the manuscript.

"Keeper of the Cats"
Romantic mystery. 4,500 words. Aimed at *Liberty* or *Cosmopolitan.* Longer

version sent on 30 November 1938 to agent Lurton Blassingame, who returned the manuscript for revision. Revised and shortened from 5,500 to 4,500 words. Tried by Blassingame at *This Week*. Non-extant.

"The Black Circle"
Adventure. 3,000 words. Longer version tried by agent Lurton Blassingame at *Short Stories* in 1938. Blassingame returned the manuscript after trying all available markets. Revised, shortened from 4,500 to 3,000 words, and retitled "The Dark Circle." Tried by agent Otis Adelbert Kline at *South Sea Stories* (fine letter in 1939, asking for more). Retitled "King Black." Tried at *Argosy* (letter from editor Rogers Terrill dated 2 June 1943).

"Shadow in the Wind"
Weird. 3,000 words.

"Dummy Act"
Mystery. 4,000 words.

"Manuscript for the Damned"
Terror. 8,000-word novelette. Aimed at *Dime Mystery Magazine* or *Horror Stories*. Tried by agent Lurton Blassingame at Popular Publications (letter from editor Rogers Terrill), *Thrilling Mystery* (letter from editor Leo Margulies in 1939), and *Startling Mystery Magazine* (letter dated 13 April 1940).

"Hall of the Devil-Flag"
Terror detective. 5,500 words. Tried by agent Lurton Blassingame at *Thrilling Mystery* (letter from editor Leo Margulies dated 9 March 1939, saying the weird angle was too slim) and *Strange Stories*. Retitled "The Satanic Flag." Retitled "Lockhart's Flag" in 1984. Sold direct to Robert M. Price on 26 April 1984, for $50.00, payable upon acceptance. Scheduled to appear in *Shudder Stories* (No. 2).

"The Caves of Malo-Oa"
Sea adventure. 6,000 words. Tried by agent Lurton Blassingame at *South Sea Stories* in 1939.

"The Return of Fabian Blair"
Terror mystery. 4,500 words. Alternate title: "Fabian Blair." Aimed at *Thrilling Mystery*. Tried by agent Lurton Blassingame at *Thrilling Mystery* (letter from editor Leo Margulies in 1939).

"Ghoul Game"
Terror mystery. 4,500 words. Aimed at *Thrilling Mystery*. Tried by agent Lurton Blassingame at *Thrilling Mystery* (letter from editor Leo Margulies in 1939).

"Borneo Lamp"
Borneo adventure. 4,000 words. Aimed at *Doc Savage*. Tried by agent Lurton Blassingame at *Doc Savage* in 1939. Revised (injecting more character play) and retitled "Light in the Jungle" in 1949. Tried at *Short Stories* in 1950.

"Pursuit to Perihelion"
Science fiction. 7,500-word novelette. Aimed at *Thrilling Wonder Stories*. Tried by agent Lurton Blassingame at *Thrilling Wonder Stories* (letter from editor Leo Margulies in 1939) and *Astonishing Stories* in 1940.

"Bride of the Tree-Men"
Borneo weird. 10,000-word novelette. Aimed at *Thrilling Mystery*. Tried by agent Lurton Blassingame at *Thrilling Mystery* (letter from editor Leo Margulies saying he

wasn't much interested in women who marry trees).

"The Wooden Parrot"''
Borneo adventure. 5,000 words. Featuring Joe Klay, the protagonist of "Deceit Post" (*Complete Stories,* February 18, 1935). Aimed at *Adventure.* Sent in 1940 to agent Lurton Blassingame, who returned the manuscript after trying all available markets. Non-extant.

"The Hand of Every"
Madagascar terror mystery. 5,500 words. Written in 1940. Aimed at *Thrilling Mystery.*

"The Cat That Had Nine Lives"
Science fantasy. Collaboration between Clifford D. Simak and Jacobi. Tried at *Thrilling Wonder Stories* in 1941. Sold direct in 1941 to *Comet,* which folded before the story could be published. Non-extant.

"Extra Wire"
Railroad adventure. 4,500 words. Tried at *Railroad Magazine* (caustic letter in 1941) and, submitted by agent Lurton Blassingame, *Short Stories* and Toronto's *Star Weekly.*

"Rawhide Evidence"
Western. 3,700 words. Sent to agent Lurton Blassingame on 11 September 1941.

"Fence Rider Fugitive"
Western. 5,000 words.

"A Letter of Marque"
Costume adventure. 6,000 words. Original version of a story eventually published as "The Commission of Captain Lace" in *Short Stories Magazine* (April, 1958).

"Jungle Rubber" (by "Jefferson Crewe")
Venezuelan adventure. 5,000 words. Aimed at *Spicy-Adventure Stories.* Tried at *Spicy-Adventure Stories* (letter dated 8 August 1943). Sold direct to Robert M. Price on 26 April 1984, for $50.00, payable upon acceptance. Scheduled to appear in *Risque Stories* (No. 2).

"Sideline Girl"
Adventure. 1,600-word short-short. Sent in 1944 to agent Lurton Blassingame, who returned the manuscript. Tried at *Liberty* (rejection slip), *Argosy* (rejection slip), *Cosmopolitan* (rejection slip), Columbia Newspaper Syndicate (brief note), and *This Week* (brief letter).

"Mono-Rail to Eternity"
Science fiction. 14,000-word novelette. Aimed at *Planet Stories.* Tried at *Planet Stories* (good letter asking for more), *Startling Stories* (nice letter), and *Amazing Stories* in 1945. Tried at *Avon Fantasy Reader* in 1947.

"The Nebula and the Necklace"
Science fiction. 12,000-word novelette. Sequel to "Enter the Nebula" (*Planet Stories,* Fall Issue, June-August, 1946). Aimed at *Planet Stories.* Tried at *Planet Stories* (letter from general manager Malcolm Reiss in 1946, requesting revision). Rewritten according to Reiss' suggestions. Tried at *Planet Stories* (letter from Reiss),

Startling Stories (letter from editor Leo Margulies), and *Amazing Stories*. Tried at *Avon Fantasy Reader* in 1947 and *Planet Stories* in 1948.

"Nine Vials of Heliotrope"
Adventure. 3,500 words. Alternate title: "The Trinidad Enigma."

Captain Royal
Costume adventure. Subtitle: *Being the Exploits of the Marquis Philip de la Darnay, who came to be known as Captain Royal, and of his service to His Majesty, Louis XIII, King of France, in the year Anno Domini 1642.* Novel begun in 1946. Two-page synopsis and first chapter.

"The Kid from Harmony"
Domestic. 4,000 words. Written 1943-1947. Aimed at *The Saturday Evening Post*. Tried at *The American* (rejection slip), *Collier's* (fine letter objecting to the ending), and *The Saturday Evening Post* (letter stating it was not quite their type of story) in 1947. Tried at *Argosy* (rejection slip), *This Week* (brief letter), *The Blue Book Magazine* (brief letter), and *Ladies' Home Journal* (fine letter asking for more and saying it had almost made it) in 1948. Tried at *Liberty* in 1949. Retitled "That Syncopated Feud" in 1959. Tried at *The Saturday Evening Post* (letter praising the writing) in 1959 and Toronto's *Star Weekly* in 1960.

"Josephine Gage"
Weird. 5,000 words. Tried at *Avon Fantasy Reader* in 1947. Sold direct to *Weird Tales* in October, 1947, but rejected in favor of "The La Prello Paper," which had been submitted at the same time. Tried at *Famous Fantastic Mysteries* in 1947. Revised. Tried at *Weird Tales* (letter from editor Dorothy McIlwraith in 1949).

"Grandmother's Writing Desk"
Domestic. 4,000 words. Tried at *Ladies' Home Journal* (nice letter dated 3 April 1949), *Today's Woman* (fine letter asking for more), *Cosmopolitan* (brief note), *Woman's Home Companion* (nice note), and Toronto's *Star Weekly*. Rewritten and retitled "The Secret Compartment" in 1958.

"A Camera for Katie"
Domestic. 3,000 words. Written in 1949.

"The Secret Passageway"
Weird. Alternate titles: "Gentleman with a Portfolio," "The House of August 36," "The Crucible of Time," "The Time Crucible," "The Golden Crucible," "The Zidesta Crucible," and "1936 August Lane." Written 1949-1950. Sent to August Derleth in 1950. Probably tried at *The Magazine of Fantasy and Science Fiction*. Revised according to Derleth's suggestions and retitled "The Crucible of Time" in 1953.

"Love's Sweet Name"
Romance. 4,500 words. Tried at *Today's Woman* and *Ladies' Home Journal* in 1951.

"The Brothers Dalfay"
Science fiction. Novelette. Sent to August Derleth in 1954. Ending rewritten according to Derleth's suggestions. Sent to agent Scott Meredith, who returned the manuscript. Revised in 1956. Tried at *Fantastic Universe* and *Super-Science Fiction* (which claimed the manuscript had been lost in the mail) in 1956. Rewritten in 1957.

"The Negative Approach"
Domestic. 4,000 words. Tried at Toronto's *Star Weekly* in 1956. Sent to agent Scott Meredith.

"Counterpart"
Science fiction. 5,000 words. Tried at *Venture Science Fiction Magazine* and probably *Short Stories Magazine* in 1958.

"The Rienza Lectures"
Science fiction. 5,000 words.

"The Second Vial"
Science fiction. Working title: "Maiden Voyage." Written 1966-1967. Tried at *Galaxy Magazine* in 1967.

The Jade Scorpion
Juvenile mystery adventure. 50,000-word novel. Working title: *Romany Camp.* Written December, 1967-winter, 1969. Sent to agent Kirby McCauley.

"The Tunnel"
Weird. 4,900 words. Sold direct first trip out to *Midnight Sun* in 1975, for $294.00, payable upon acceptance, but the magazine ceased publication before the story could be used. Sent to agent Kirby McCauley.

"Offspring"
Weird. 4,500 words. Working title: "Levitations in Lavender." Sold first trip out by agent Kirby McCauley to Neal R. Blaikie (publisher of the 1977 chapbook, *Carl Jacobi: An Appreciation),* for a magazine Blaikie never put out.

"A Letter to Sarah"
Domestic. 2,500 words. Sent to agent Kirby McCauley.

" A Quire of Foolscap"
Weird. 3,000 words. Sent to agent Kirby McCauley.

Appendix II
Selected Letters to Carl Jacobi

94 Montgomery Street,
Pawtucket, Rhode Island.

Dear Mr. Jacobi,

Whether or not it is ethical to
express sincere appreciation of such a letter as
yours, I don't know. In fact, I don't know either
if such letters as yours are entirely ethical in
the first place, especially among the writing
profession. Writers, you know, are supposed to
be a jealous, stiff-necked lot, with high-flung
noses constantly in the air.

But I do know that your letter
brought me more real pleasure than any check I
have yet received for any story I have yet written.
"Fan notes" come to me occasionally, many of them
sloppy with praise and many others heavy with
criticism. As yet, I've never received one that
gave a decent reason for either the praise or
the knock. And as yet, I haven't been honored
with a complimentary letter from a fellow writer.
I thank you. I thank you also for being specific
enough to state why you liked the stories in
question.

I've seen some of your stories in
WEIRD TALES, I believe, though I don't write for
that magazine myself and consequently don't study
the material therein. However, I spend a good bit
of my time browsing about the news-stands, peering
at contents pages, and wondering when my own name
will appear often enough to attract attention! I
remember seeing your work. At least, I'm under
the impression that I do.

Incidentally, I'm no hardened professional
myself. Like you, I wrote for college and school
publications and soon discovered that I liked to
write. Landed a job soon after as "literary editor",
reviewing books that I didn't have time to read.
Sold my first two stories (terrible ones, at that) to
ACTION STORIES, and threw up the job the next day.
Went broke twice, bought a car with my next check (from
the old regime of BRIEF STORIES) and found myself
stranded in Boston with a forty-dollar-a-month apartment
on my hands.

That was a year ago. Since you may be
looking for friendly encouragement, I'll give you the
rest of the story. I went to New York, broke an arm
cranking the car one morning, returned to Pawtucket,
and hired three musty rooms on the top floor of an
abandoned shack. Lovely setting for the creation of
masterpieces, according to popular belief! The masterpieces weren't forthcoming, but I did manage to start
the "Tsiang House" yarns and persuade R. de S. Horn of
SHORT STORIES that they were worth printing. And
now, thanks to that same magazine and half a dozen
others, including TRIPLE-X, HIGH SPOT, TOP NOTCH,

2

BRIEF STORIES, ASTOUNDING, and some of the juvenile and
household magazines, I'm moving along at a fairly
decent rate of speed. It isn't so bad after all, and
it certainly was worth the early effort.

You know me now as well as I know myself.
All this, of course, is more or less confidential.
I'm sure you'll treat it as such. Your letter was
so open and friendly in itself that it could be
answered only in this way.

Hope I'll hear from you again. If you
should chance on more of my attempts at fiction,
I hope you'll be inclined to let me know what
you think of them. Criticism is the greatest help
you and I can unearth, you know. We have no "boss"
to point out the dust in the corner, and editors
rarely find time to make more than their own personal
objections.

As for my knowledge of Borneo, whether
or not I've been there is "none of yer business, feller"!
However, if you are inclined to write South Seas stories,
or yarns with a Borneo setting, I heartily recommend
O'Brien's "Faery Lands in the South Seas" and William
Beebe's books of Borneo travel.

Do let's hear from you again.

Truly yours,

Hugh B. Cave

August 14, 1930

Incidentally, I no longer live in the three musty
rooms. If you should happen to be touring the country
this summer, the door of my apartment is wide open for
you.

And another, very important thing; old man: Have you
thought of dropping a note to the editors of SHORT
STORIES and ASTOUNDING STORIES, and telling them what
you think of my stuff? It's a mercenary thing to ask,
I know; but such letters insure future checks and keep
the home fires sizzling! Being one of your fellow
workers, I'd surely appreciate such an act.

Jacobi's first letter from Hugh B. Cave (14 August 1930)

Weird Tales

REGISTERED IN U.S. PATENT OFFICE

A MAGAZINE of the   BIZARRE and UNUSUAL

840 N. Michigan Ave.   Chicago, Ill.

EDITORIAL ROOMS

January 9, 1932.

Mr. Carl Jacobi
3717- Fourth Avenue, So.
Minneapolis, Minn.

Dear Mr. Jacobi:

     I have given a careful re-reading to
THE MAN FROM MAKASSAR. I regret to say
that the story, although it has its points
of excellence, still seems unconvincing, and
there is too much left up in the air. Sorry,
but that is my reaction to the story.

     Did you ever revise that story about
the strange book and the vampire woman in the
strange house-- a German vampire, I believe
it was? That story still haunts me. If you
have touched it up since then I would like to
see it again.

              Sincerely yours,

              Farnsworth Wright,
FW:MM.   Editor

From Farnsworth Wright (9 January 1932)

Dear Mr.Jacobi:

I found your recent letter very interesting,and if my comments on your story "Mive",have helped you with the editors,I am sincerely glad. I consider that story as one of the finest of its kind I have ever read. I am glad to hear that you have placed a story with Oriental Stories,and shall watch for it.
I shall also look for "The Curse Pistol" in Strange Tales. It was not my fortune to read either of the other stories you mentioned; in fact,I live so far out of civilization,as it were,that I cant keep track of the magazines very well. Its forty miles to the nearest first-class news-stand,so my magazine reading is rather desultory
I hope you sell those stories upon which you mentioned y were working — also hope you like my yarn in the forthcoming Weird Tale
hoping to hear from you again,at your leisure,I am,

Cordially,

Robert E. Howard

From Robert E. Howard (postmarked 22 March 1932)

Sauk City
Wisconsin
5   April

Dear Carl,

I haven't yet read the May issue of W. T., beyond the shorts,
and I can't say that I cared much for either The Bishop Sees
Through or The Broken Thread. I must confess also that I didn't
like the illustration for The Brotherhood of Blood, nor did I
care for the fragments of the story I read here and there. However, that must of necessity mean comparatively little, for I
am forced because of my tremendous reading to judge stories
largely by how they could have been handled better, or by literary style, and so forth. Cave is not a writer of the first
water. None of his work that I've seen compares with H. P.'s,
Smith's (whose address, by the way is simply, Auburn, California),
Whitehead's, nor even with my own good group (of which you've
read only The Panelled Room, will read shortly The Sheraton Mirror). Cave is essentially, like Howard, the action story writer,
and is at his best with action on a minimum of atmospheric background, though Cave is to be commended for the accuracy of his
backgrounds. Yet it may be that what I have read of his work
has not been of his best. I look forward to Stragella which
comes out within a day or two.

What almost sent me into hysteria in this issue of W. T. was the
blurb for In the Left Wing -- Wright gives the entire story away,
and save for the diction, no one need read it after the first page
or so. But it doesn't matter ultimately. The story will probably
be very well liked. If Howard has a fight between a vampire and
a man, I think it's stupid. He can't seem to be getting anywhere
without a fight or so; why in hell doesn't he write for the action
magazines?

Re Whitehead's style -- don't make the mistake of classifying him
with the more ordinary writer, Carl. What you are evidently doing
is comparing his stories, with their greater emphasis on character
and atmosphere, with the definitely inferior tales that emphasize
plot. I liked The Trap (save for title) best in the March S. T.,
The Tiger second best.

If you've been travelling about the state, why not take a drive
down to Sauk City -- if you've a machine that is. You could make
this burg in 7 hours following your U. S. highway 12 all the way,
and could stay a day or two or more, and drive back again. It's
a nice drive, too. Think it over.

Good luck with all your stories. I did show Moss Island to H. P.,
and he wrote as follows: "Thanks exceedingly for Moss Island, which
is pretty effective despite prosaic lapses and a plethora of tech-
nicality. The climactic portions develop magnificently. Jacobi
really has phenomenal talent, and ought to be well worth watching
during the years to come." To which I may add that whatever talent
you have, may well be spoiled by giving too great attention to the
plot-action story and thus over-emphasising it to your detriment.

11.

What I mean is simply this: few great books are action stories,
ditto few great stories -- probably one out of every 5000. It is
okeh to work in action for profit, but one must always realise
its actual worth. Thus I say that of all my weirds published, no
one is thus far really worth preserving.

Re knowing when your stories will appear: if they're long ones,
they are scheduled three months before appearing, which accounts
for both In the Left Wing and The Lair of the Star-Spawn. Of cou
Wright always tells me that, naturally, as he will you, too, when
he has scheduled your stories. The shorter ones he can't tell ab
until about 45 days before date of issue, since they are fillers
serted to take up a certain space only. Re The Sheraton Mirror;
asked Wright to schedule this in either the Sept or Oct because I
wanted it to be eligible for inclusion in an anthology of weirds
to be issued next January. Not that it will necessarily be. Bat
doesn't tell one anything, but when he has more than one story by
an author (when any editor has, for that matter), he usually does
let more than two issues of a mag slip past without a story by th
author. If the May doesn't have The Thing etc., then the July ce
tainly will have.

Yes, I agree that there's room for a deductive detective in the
pulps -- but the editors don't. However, Bierman is continuing t
hold The Adventure of the Norcross Riddle -- what for, I don't
know. Probably the best published Pons tale from a point of writing was The Adventure of the Late Mr. Faversham, but the Black
Cardinal didn't lag far behind. These tales were both mild sa-
tires, of which the editors were blissfully unconscious.

I agree with you anent the title They Shall Rise in Great Numbers
and have shortened it to They Shall Rise. I had intended to call
it that in the first place, but I thought it would be too similar
to two of my already published weird titles to get by -- He Shall
Come, and Those Who Seek -- but I've changed my mind. Wright rejected it, not liking the story, though Bates and Clayton had bot
decided to take it at one time, but Clayton went back on his de-
cision at the last minute -- after the ms. was already marked for
the printer! Those things happen, worse luck.

Meanwhile, I've just written a short-short detective yarn, The Ma
Who Was God, which probably won't land anywhere either. Trouble
with me is that I've got too good a detective-fiction background
to produce action crap well enough to get by with it. However,
I'm sending it to Real Detective, whose editor has been plaguing
me for something, despite the fact that he's got a short of mine
to run yet.

as always,

August

From August Derleth (5 April 1932)

Auburn, Cal.

June 16th, 1932.

My dear Carl Jacobi:

I was glad to hear from you, and had meant to acknowledge your letter more promptly.

Indeed, I liked your "Mive" very much, and thought it an almost perfect gem of strange and malign fantasy. I enjoyed "Moss Island" also. I am glad that Wright has taken some more of your work, and will look for it in W.T. I don't imagine my praise by itself would influence Wright very much--though he is certainly amenable to anything approaching a quorum.

I'll also anticipate your tale in S.T. I too am damnably sorry that the magazine has had to cut down its issues, since we need it badly as an alternative medium to W.T. Bates and Wright seem to balance each other rather nicely--what one doesn't like the other often will. It may interest you to know that three of my yarns in S.T. had previously been turned down by Wright. Another of his rejections is now being considerd very favorably by Bates. On the other hand, some of B.'s rejections ("The Maker of Gargoyles" is an instance) have been taken by W.

Good luck! and let me hear from you again some time.

Cordially,

Clark Ashton Smith

From Clark Ashton Smith (16 June 1932)

Weird Tales

REGISTERED IN U.S. PATENT OFFICE

A MAGAZINE of the BIZARRE and UNUSUAL

840 N. Michigan Ave.   Chicago, Ill.

EDITORIAL ROOMS

February 14, 1933

Mr. Carl R. Jacobi
3717 Fourth Avenue So.
Minneapolis, Minn.

Dear Mr. Jacobi:

    We are reserving the right to broadcast a dramatiz-
ation of REVELATIONS IN BLACK by radio, if the story
lends itself to such dramatization. This will apply to
all future stories of yours published in WEIRD TALES;
but if we receive any money from such broadcasting of
your stories, it will be turned over to you.

    We have just completed negotiations to have 52
radio dramatizations of stories from WEIRD TALES broadcast nationally, for the purpose of advertising the magazine. These broadcasts will not be on a chain hook-up,
but will be broadcast by the stations individually from
electrical transcriptions made in Hollywood. All money
that we may receive from such broadcasting will be turned
over to the authors, as our interest lies only in increasing sales through the publicity thus obtained.

    The first broadcast (DE BRIGNAC'S LADY, by Kirk
Mashburn) will have William Farnum, Viola Dana and Wallace
Reid, Jr. in the cast.

Sincerely yours,
Farnsworth Wright,
Editor.

FW:RG

Cross Plains,Texas,
Saint Patrick's Day, 1933.

Dear Mr. Jacobi:

I am glad to write to Wright, commenting
favorably on "Revelations in Black". It is an unusual and
well written story, reflecting the same imaginative quality
which caught my attention in "Mive". Frankly, you have
an imagination of a subtle and poetic nature rarely met with,
and should go far in the writing profession.

Thanks for the things you said about my work.
I'm glad you liked "The Scarlet Citadel" so well.

I'm sorry you suffered from the collapse of
Strange Tales. I, too, had a story with the company which was returned unpublished and unpaid for.

Yes, Derleth told me that Wright had accepted
another Lovecraft tale, which is good news for all lovers of
the weird story.

With best wishes,

Cordially,

Robert E. Howard.

From Robert E. Howard (postmarked 18 March 1933)

In replying please address

The *Hydrographer*,

Admiralty.

London, S.W.1.

quoting **H   4606/33.**

Hydrographic Department,

Admiralty,

London, S.W.1.

31st July, 1933.

Sir,

In reply to your letter of the 21st June, I have
to inform you that this Department has no knowledge of
any island named Tiger or of a Longan Archipelago in the
position given in your letter.   There is, however, a
Longan Island in the Ninigo or l'Echiquier Islands in
latitude 1°13'S., longitude 144°18'E. (approximately).

An island named Tiger was reported by Captain
Bristow in 1817 to exist in latitude 1°45'S., longitude
142°19'E., but in 1894 information was received from the
German Government that no island existed in this position,
and that the so-called Tiger Island was probably identical
with Matty Island, now known as Wuvulu, which was discovered
by Cartaret in 1767, and which lies in latitude 1°46'S.,
longitude 142°56'E.

There is a plan of Wuvulu Island on a scale of
1/50,000 on Chart No. 613, published by the German
Admiralty; apart from this, nothing can be added to the
scanty information concerning the island, which is contained
in Pacific Islands Pilot, Volume I, 6th Edition, 1933,
which can be obtained from the Admiralty Chart Agent,
J. D. Potter, and any of the sub-agencies in America.

I am, Sir,

Your obedient Servant,

Captain, R.N.,
for Hydrographer.

Carl Jacobi,
3717, Fourth Avenue South,
Minneapolis,
Minnesota,
U. S. A.

From Hydrographic Department, Admiralty, London (31 July 1933)

Weird Tales

— REGISTERED IN U.S. PATENT OFFICE —

A MAGAZINE of the BIZARRE and UNUSUAL

840 N. Michigan Ave.   **Chicago, Ill.**

EDITORIAL ROOMS

June 6, 1934

Mr. Carl Jacobi
3717 Fourth Ave. S.
Minneapolis, Minn.

Dear Mr. Jacobi:

I am reconsidering my rejection of CELAENO, although
I do not think you have changed it much. When I rejected
this story, I did so because it was not explained how these
monsters of ancient Greek mythology came to an English
estate, and how they had survived during the intervening
centuries without being seen by man. But on rereading the
story, I think the last page provides an answer by the
doubt that it raises as to whether Mr. Bumpstead was the
victim of hallucinations.

We can offer you eighty dollars on publication for
CELAENO.

We are reserving the right to broadcast a radio
adaptation of CELAENO after the story is published, if it
lends itself to such adaptation; but in case we receive
any money from such broadcast, it will be turned over to
you. Our purpose will be fully served by the publicity
attendant on such broadcast.

In accordance with your request, I am returning THREE
BRASS CUBES, which was accepted for the MAGIC CARPET MAGAZINE.
Your manuscript had been prepared for the printer before we
decided to suspend publication temporarily.

2

Weird Tales

REGISTERED IN U.S. PATENT OFFICE

A MAGAZINE of the   BIZARRE and UNUSUAL

840 N. Michigan Ave.   Chicago,

EDITORIAL ROOMS

Can you not suggest a more appealing title than CE

THE SATANIC PIANO was well received by our readers it was not in the running for favorite story. Moore's LET DREAM and Howard's QUEEN OF THE BLACK COAST had the all to themselves for most popular story in the May iss

REVELATIONS IN BLACK was very popular; in fact, it second only to SHAMBLEAU in popularity among all the st we printed in 1933.

Best regards.

Sincerely yours,

FW:RG   Wright.
eno.

From Farnsworth Wright (6 June 1934)

Long Nawang den 15en September 1934.

Dear Sir,

In reply to your letter of 6th Februari, I
am glad to be able to tell you something about the country here.
First I should like to inform you that no man yet has
stationed here,whereas there isnt any business to do.The post
is to far in the interior and there are to much troubles to
get things up here.Regarding your correspondence there is no
trouble at all,for every officer of the Royal Netherlanth Indies
Army knows the English Language,though not every one knows it
perfectly well.As all officers only stay here for one or two
years,the best thing you can do is to address always to the
officer in charge.
I don't know the book written by Carl Lumholtz .In that
time military transports came up the river Mahakam.But as that
river was to bad,one changed the way to Long Nawang years ago.
Nowadays transports come up the river Kajan from Boelongan,
a small harbourplace at the East -Cost of Borneo.These transports leave Boelongan(also calledTandjong-Selor) once a month.
Aftergooing up the river about two months they reach Long Nawang.
The transport-s exist of several prahus special build
for the mighty rapids that are to be surmouted,rowed by Dajak
people from here(Kenja's).
Motorboats cannot be used on the Kajanriver.
Every evening one makes bivouac at the riverside.
The hole yourney goes through the jungle.Weeks after weeks
one doesnot see any people,as there are no native villages un-
till near Long Nawang.
All things one takes along with,has to be packed very well
in soldered tins,to protect them again rain- and riverwater.
and even manytimes gets things here moistened or entirely de-
stbyed.
Arriving in Tandjong Selor (by steamer of the "K(oninklyke)
P(akketvaart) M(aatscappy)") from Soerabajaa or Bandjermasin,
you have to look for prahus ,rowers a boy who can cook and than
care for your things(luggage).
Besides your campbed one has to bring with a mosquito net
("klamboe") of very close texture,for there are millions of
small insects(agas) which sting more violent than misquitos.
Than one has to take along livehood for two monthes.The
best thing to do is to take along rice,salt,fryoil,dry fish,tea
some sugar and a few tins.But these are havy and take much place.
The onderafdeeling here (district) is called "Apo Kajan"
The climate is cool(575 meter above sealevel)Principaldeseases
are malaria and dyssentery.Nearly everyone has to get several
attacks of the last one,which are sometimes very severe.Last
year I got one enduring 5 months.
The charming native people is living in long houses existing
of several rooms.Each room is destined for one or moer familys.
All villages are build on the riverside.In the Apo Kajan are the
rivers the ways.Though there are very primitive native pathes.

In the jungle one meets a lot of bloodsuckers,so "shorts" arent
used if one goes on foot.we use nailed shoes,half of them made of
linen.In the prahus one can use tennisshoes.
    The post only exist outof the garrison.There are three officers,
the captaincommander,a lieutenant and a army medical officer.
    Ther are no stores here,so things one need,one has to bring
with.
    Natives are fond of Java tobacco,beads and other things,wich
one can get in Tandjong Selor.

    I am sorry that this letter will reach you so late.I got yours
in tne last days of Bali and had not time till yet to answeryou.
  · If you reply,your letter perhaps will not reach me personelly,
for it may be I will leave Long Nawang in November.But I am sure
my succeeder will give you any informations you will ask for.

    Hoping that you will not mind all my mistakes(I did not speak
or write English for years) I am

                                    very sincerely yours,

From commanding officer, Long Nawang, Borneo (15 September 1934)

Dear Mr. Jacobi,

Your letter arrived at Ambunti today per
Chu Leong's pinnace which trades between Madang and the Sepik
River, sometimes (as today) coming as far as this post with sundry
mail and a few stores. On such occasions there is a good deal of
festivity. We don't often see pinnaces.

Ambunti is 230 odd miles from the Sepik
mouth in the Mandated Territory of New Guinea, and not in Papua.
Papua has belonged to Australia ever since she pinched it from
the Papuans. The Territory belonged to the Germans until the
end of the great War, when Great Britain, who is rather good at that
sort of thing, took charge of it, holding that those who butcher
babies and rape Red Cross Nurses are not fit to govern a primitive
people.

There are only two whites stationed at
Ambunti now, Lieut. Colonel Woodman D.S.O. and G.A.E. Reading Unfinished B.A.

In addition there are 17 police boys and
I Corporal, also I Doctor Boy who wears a peaked cap with a red
cross on it and a 'lap-lap' (short loin cloth) of white with a red
hem and another large red cross. The police boys on parade wear
khaki short trousers, tunic, and cap. On patrol they abandon this
uniform for khaki lap-lap and cap. They are supplied with .303
service rifles and it hasn't occured to them yet to bump us all off.

Our work at Ambunti consists mainly of
collecting head tax from controlled villages, settling native-
disputes, checking tribal fighting, making contact with uncontrolled
villages, sending in monthly returns to the District Headquarters
at Wewak, and shooting 'nat-nats' (mosquitoes) with antiquated
spray guns.

The nat-nats are unbelievably bad and
mostly oenophilenes (I think that's how you spell it), the
malaria carrying mosquitoes. These are small and black and stand
on their heads to bite. To prevent infection we take five to ten
grains of quinine a day, which isn't really a preventive at all,
but it minimises the severity of the dose when we do catch it.

We also take quinine capsules with us when
we go on furlough. They make fair to middling contraceptives.

The climate here? Well, I suppose there's
not much use telling you it is hot. But believe me it is hot -
as hot as hell. Humidity is very high and the heat is a clammy
wet steamy heat. You are always bathed in sweat, especially after
'kai-kai' (food, and so - a meal) or a hot cup of tea. How is the
time of the rains. That helps a little, but not much. The Sepik
is flooded and many villages on its banks are completely under
water and the inhabitants live with their pigs, dogs, etc in their
huts. They travel from house to house in canoes, the bows of
which are invariably carved in the form of a crocodiles head.

Nearly every night Ambunti is visited with
an electrical thunderstorm, sometimes accompanied by rain,
sometimes not. When it rains it doesn't piddle.

But taken all in all the weather here isn't
nearly so bad as people unacquainted with tropical conditions are
apt to imagine. At all events it doesn't kill us. Moreover the
Administration makes a policy of sending its officials to Ambunti
for short periods. Mr. Woodman was here in 1929 for two years, the
longest anyone has stayed here. He has been sent back this year for
a further term. He hopes to Christ it isn't for two more years.

Ambunti is situated on a small hill facing a stretch
of the river about six hundred yards long. On each side is
a 'sac-sac' (sago palm) swamp. We have plenty of fruit -
paw-paw, pineapples, bananas (including a variety with red
skins), coconuts, 'muli's (a fruit like lemons). The natives
of Sepik villages live largely on yam and sac-sac, which is
obtained by crushing the stem of a sac-sac palm. Working sac-sac
is the expression used for this operation.
About 8 miles upstream is the village of Yambon,
3 miles downstream Malu. Both are large villages, able to muster
over a hundred fighting men.
Malu on many occasions has threatened to wipe out
Ambunti. The tragedy of it (and believe me it is a tragedy if
you are here on the spot) is that they could do it any time
they wanted. When we are asleep, for instance. We can't keep
guards posted all the time.
About three years ago they stood within 3 feet of the
man who was in charge here at the time while he had a smoke.
They were waiting for him to go to bed. Instead he went down to
the village on another mission and in a scuffle a police boy
shot a kanaka. The villagers thought their plan was known
and let their planned attack fall through.
And that is the way we have to work now. Bluff them.
Let them think we are abreast of all their moves. And above all
make them think we are not afraid of them.
But on the whole we have little trouble from the
nearby villages - Timbonki, Avatip , Malu, Yambon, Brugnui,
Waskuk etc. and I personally am inclined to think the trouble
with the Malus is over-rated.
A days walk away we have villages that have never
been visited by white men.
The villages themselves stretch along the bank of
the River, and are long and narrow. The houses are built on
piles about five feet off the ground, roofed with 'maratan', and
the ceiling is very close to the floor. There are no windows
and only one small hole for the door. The natives sleep in
woven baskets - as a safe guard against nat-nats.
The centre of village life is the 'House Tambaran' -
(tambaran is a word meaning spirit) - in which are kept the
secret things on which only the initiates may look.
The chief of the village is called the Luluai. The
spokesman the Tultul. Other big men are the those in charge of
the House Tambaran and sorcerers. In the middle Sepik between
Origambi and the River there is a strong secret society for
called 'SangumanKK'. They practise killing, the motive of which
is not understood yet.
Headhunting is still carried on in villages not
yet under control. In controlled villages as far as we know it
has finished.
The biggest pests on the River, apart from mosquitoes
are the missionaries
I hope I have given you sufficient local colour for
your story or article or whatever it is you propose doing.
If I can do more I shall only be too pleased.
If at any time you you lay your hands on a spare
copy of 'Esquire', 'New Yorker', or 'Hooley', or anything at all
that is either (1) full of sex and nude women (2) of fairly high
standard or (3) both, I should be very grateful to you if after you
have finished with it you should bung it along to Ambunti.

(3)

p.s.   Don't think the Doctor Boy I mentioned earlier is
     a doctor . He knows how to tie a bandage and that is about
all.
     Vegetation along the Sepik consists mostly of sacsac,
'pit-pit' (wild sugar cane), 'kapiak' trees (massive with large
leaves), kango (a sort of water-cress - it makes good eating),
D'Alberti vine (hanging to the kapiaks, and with a magnificent
deep red flower the size of your two palms), coconuts (near
the villages), and tall kunai grass (about 6, 7, 8, 9, or 10
feet high)
     Vegetation doesn't overhang the river because the
river is nearly a mile wide for hundreds of miles. At the
time of the 'dry water' there are to be seen thousands of
crocodiles on the mud banks. During high water they retreat
back into the swamps.
     The villages send 'talk' by means of garamuts, large
carven hollow logs, which they 'fight' with poles. These
can be heardv for miles - Bom.... Bom....Bom Bom....etc.
     For sing-sings they beat kundus, smaller
drums shaped like hour glasses with flat ends over which
is drawn tight skin. They hold these in one hand and beat
them with the palm of the other.

The government official is
called the "Kiap" by the natives,
who are born thieves, though
in their own code highly
moral people.

pps I too was a journalist
before I came up here (a
damn bad one I might
add).

From commanding officer, Ambunti, New Guinea (29 March 1937)

Group
ntures
ective
ve
tery
Stories
orts
stern
r Stories
rs
ers
gle
ology
Western
Magazine
lective
etective
ve
orts
tern
ances
ctive

STANDARD MAGAZINES, INC.

AND BETTER PUBLICATIONS, INC.

22 WEST 48TH STREET

NEW YORK CITY

COLLEGE HUMOR
•
Mechanics & Handicre
•
COLLEGE LIFE
✓
Cable Address
"MAGSTAND"

October 6th, 1938

Mr. Carl Jacobi
3717-4th Avenue
Minneapolis, Minn.

Dear Mr. Jacobi:

Are you getting too much sleep? Are your
nerves too steady? Does your heart beat regularly
and monotonously?

If so, here's a chance to snap out of it
and scare yourself into a fit. THRILLING MYSTERY is
in the market for some short stories, up to six thousand
words--and I'd like you to take a crack at one or two.
But remember, they have to be good enough to make you
shiver and perspire when you're through! The old
THRILLING MYSTERY stuff--I mean the feeling and atmosphere, and not the theme, of course. Some fresh angles
are always welcome, you know.

You guys seem to have forgotten all about T.M.--
it's still a cent-a-worder, too.

Sincerely yours,

LEO MARGULIES
Editorial Director

lm:hr

From Leo Margulies (6 October 1938)

T. SCOTT
sident

MALCOLM REISS
General Manager

FICTION HOUSE, Inc.

Publishers

670 FIFTH AVENUE

NEW YORK 19, N. Y.

June 27, 1945

Dear Mr. Jacobi,

When I reached the climax of TEPONDICON, all I could say was, "This Carl Jacobi is a bas——." Then I thought it over and decided, "What if our readers do ask for their money back?"

In other words, you can list the above title on your record of sales. If you'll drop me an okay, I'll put through a check for $50.00.

Regarding future submissions, I'm not too keen on "Grannie Annie", but a sequel to "Enter The Nebula" will be okay, if the story you turn out packs a wallop - suspense, characterization and action, background and mood.

I'll be looking forward to seeing your next effort on my desk.

Cordially,

Chet Whitehorn, Editor
PLANET STORIES

From Chet Whitehorn (27 June 1945)

9 ROCKEFELLER PLAZA
NEW YORK 20. N. Y.

OFFICE OF THE EDITOR

July 21, 1949

Mr. Carl Jacobi
3717 - 4th Ave., S.
Minneapolis, Minn.

Dear Mr. Jacobi:

We don't seem to have had anything from
you lately for WEIRD. I realize we are not a large
or lucrative market, but, generally speaking, we
are an enthusiastic one. Try us with a story before
too long a time, won't you?

Sincerely,

WEIRD TALES

Dorothy McIlwraith
Editor

DMcI:pc

From Dorothy McIlwraith (21 July 1949)

Index